Coping with Burnout

Originally from the UK, Donna Andronicos lives in New Zealand, and brings a wealth of experience and understanding to her work as a trainer, leadership coach and writer. As a keynote speaker and MC, she is often described as 'entertaining, motivating, inspiring and energizing'. A natural storyteller, Donna skilfully blends her credible insights with a mixture of humour and down-to-earth practicality, in a way that engages her audience in all aspects of her work and writing. A former consultant, with an extensive career working with leading organizations in the UK, New Zealand and Asia, Donna is passionate about helping others to move beyond their personal and professional barriers in life.

Overcoming Common Problems Series

Selected titles

A full list of titles is available from Sheldon Press,
36 Causton Street, London SW1P 4ST and on our website at
www.sheldonpress.co.uk

The Book of Body Language
David Cohen

The Complete Carer's Guide
Bridget McCall

The Confidence Book
Gordon Lamont

Coping Successfully with Period Problems
Mary-Claire Mason

Coping with Age-related Memory Loss
Dr Tom Smith

Coping with Chemotherapy
Dr Terry Priestman

Coping with Compulsive Eating
Ruth Searle

Coping with Diverticulitis
Peter Cartwright

Coping with Family Stress
Dr Peter Cheevers

Coping with Hearing Loss
Christine Craggs-Hinton

Coping with Heartburn and Reflux
Dr Tom Smith

Coping with Macular Degeneration
Dr Patricia Gilbert

Coping with Radiotherapy
Dr Terry Priestman

Coping with Tinnitus
Christine Craggs-Hinton

The Depression Diet Book
Theresa Cheung

Depression: Healing Emotional Distress
Linda Hurcombe

Depressive Illness
Dr Tim Cantopher

The Fertility Handbook
Dr Philippa Kaye

Helping Children Cope with Anxiety
Jill Eckersley

How to Approach Death
Julia Tugendhat

How to be a Healthy Weight
Philippa Pigache

How to Get the Best from Your Doctor
Dr Tom Smith

How to Make Life Happen
Gladeana McMahon

How to Talk to Your Child
Penny Oates

The IBS Healing Plan
Theresa Cheung

Living with Autism
Fiona Marshall

Living with Eczema
Jill Eckersley

Living with Heart Failure
Susan Elliot-Wright

Living with Loss and Grief
Julia Tugendhat

Living with a Seriously Ill Child
Dr Jan Aldridge

The Multiple Sclerosis Diet Book
Tessa Buckley

Overcoming Emotional Abuse
Susan Elliot-Wright

Overcoming Hurt
Dr Windy Dryden

The PMS Handbook
Theresa Cheung

Simplify Your Life
Naomi Saunders

Stress-related Illness
Dr Tim Cantopher

The Thinking Person's Guide to Happiness
Ruth Searle

The Traveller's Good Health Guide
Dr Ted Lankester

Treat Your Own Knees
Jim Johnson

Treating Arthritis – The Drug-Free Way
Margaret Hills

Overcoming Common Problems

Coping with Burnout

DONNA ANDRONICOS

First published in Great Britain in 2007

Sheldon Press
36 Causton Street
London SW1P 4ST

British Library Cataloguing-in-Publication Data
A catalogue record for this book is available from the British Library

ISBN 978–1–84709–025–6

1 3 5 7 9 10 8 6 4 2

Typeset by Fakenham Photosetting Ltd, Fakenham, Norfolk
Printed in Great Britain by Ashford Colour Press

Produced on paper from sustainable forests

Contents

Acknowledgements

Thanks first and foremost to all of you who shared your stories of burnout with me. You gave me insight as well as inspiration.

To Rachel, Alison, Jan, Bridget, Suzanne, Richard, Shane, Nev, and Wendy Darling; thanks to all of you for your unconditional support and love (and for responding to all of those obscure text messages during the creation of this book). You are my rocks.

I'd also like to send out a big thank you to all of those stress gurus who have travelled the road before me. Without you, we'd probably all still be sitting in the dark eating fat food and wondering what to do next.

Thanks also to Zenith Publishing and Sheldon Press for editing this book before it was unleashed on to the public.

And finally, to Chester and Liddy, a promise kept.

Preface

Burnout is a devastating experience that can feel as if you're spiralling deeper and deeper into a black hole with no way of stopping your descent. I know, because I've been there. In March 2005 I realized I was suffering from burnout. It had taken me a couple of years to get there and for five months I didn't even know what was happening – until I hit the wall. Once the reality set in, the emotions I experienced ranged from immense sadness and grief, to shame, failure, embarrassment and anger, mostly at myself for letting things get this far.

I had lost my passion for the work that I loved, lost my direction and, I felt, lost my credibility as a coach. Who was I to be offering to help others when I couldn't even get my own act together? My self-confidence was at an all-time low and I didn't know who to turn to for help.

It was during those dark days that I had an epiphany, in – of all places – the kitchen, as I sat on the floor crying. It was a moment that turned what could have been a devastating experience into a gift. You see, I believe that everything happens to us for a reason, and this train of thought led me to conclude that, given my line of work, perhaps I was experiencing burnout in order to understand it better, and thereby help others through it. This thought was what enabled me to get through the worst of my burnout in three months. During this time I observed and explored my own experience and experimented with different approaches to my recovery, and came to understand burnout better as an apparently harsh but effective life teacher, teaching me some valuable life skills, such as learning how to prioritize my time and energy more effectively; how to move beyond stressful or negative situations quickly; and how to have the ability to recognize my stress triggers early on and to adapt my response and actions accordingly.

A further three months later, I had well and truly got my energy and zest for life back and, armed with my new knowledge and experiential understanding of my strange new friend, I started to talk to others who had had similar experiences. Through these confidential interviews, I found that the average time for most people to come through burnout appeared to be somewhere between six months and a year; that some relapsed back into burnout again within six months of their first experience; and that many common characteristics seemed to exist, not only in the various stages being experienced, but also in the ways in which people handled stress following their experience of burnout.

One of the results of all this work has been this book, which documents the approach I used during my own experience of burnout, supported by a selection of the knowledge I gained during this time, as well as quotes from some of the interviews I had with others (printed with their kind permission and with the names of each person changed to retain confidentiality). The opinions expressed in this book have not been designed to be a substitute for professional help in any way, but to complement it.

Hence the title *Coping with Burnout*, which aims to guide you through burnout in a practical way, bit by bit, rather than weighing you down with what you may already know about stress and stress-related disorders. There's already a wealth of information available on these two topics, and I have no desire to try to reinvent the wheel.

You'll have your own reasons for picking up this book. Perhaps you're concerned that you may be heading for burnout yourself and you want to find a way of slamming the brakes on before you get there; you may be helping a loved one through their experience; or you may just be curious about the topic. Whatever your reasons, this is my gift to you, and I hope with all my heart that you find something within its pages that helps you at this time.

Introduction

Topic Teasers

- Have you come to accept a permanent state of exhaustion as being 'normal' in your life?
- Do you rely on coffee and sugar fixes to get you through the day?
- Do you suffer from illnesses whenever you take time out?
- Can you remember what it feels like not to be this way?

Is this book for me?

If you're still trying to decide whether or not to buy or read this book, you may also be asking yourself some questions. For this reason, I've taken a stab at guessing what might be meandering through the space between your ears at this time.

Who is this book for?

Coping with Burnout is for those who want to:

- remember what it feels like not to feel tired all the time;
- be able to proactively identify the warning signs of prolonged stress and/or energy imbalance;
- understand how the world around them, and how they interact with that world, may be influencing their stress levels and how they feel on a daily basis;
- be able to prioritize change in their lives and ultimately reduce their stress levels;
- learn how to increase their overall energy levels and engagement with life.

So is this just another book about work–life balance?

No. It's about learning how to effectively manage and sustain your energy across all areas of your life; how to recognize the signs of prolonged stress/energy imbalance and how to avoid their inevitable consequences (i.e. burnout); how to identify the external factors that may be influencing your stress/energy levels; and what can happen internally when we get the balance wrong.

If it's not about work–life balance, what does it cover?

At the beginning of the book I've provided my own interpretation of the relationship that I feel exists between stress and burnout. Armed with this theory, you'll be off to explore the many factors of your external world, the role of the 'energy vampire', and the intricate mechanics of your internal energy centre. And finally, by working through the questions in each chapter, you'll be ready to pull together your own Action Plan for change.

Will this book give me step-by-step instructions on what to do?

Yes and no. The book is designed as a guide to provide you with assessments, questions and action-planning sections to help you to make the necessary changes in your life, but how, when and if you make these changes will be entirely up to you. After all, it will be *your* insights and motivation to take action that will initiate any changes you decide to make, not mine.

So what approach do you use?

I've adopted a 'coaching' style for this book. In other words, I haven't set out to provide you with all of the answers. Instead, I've tried to stimulate your thought process by providing you with information and questions that will help you to reach your own conclusions about the course of action you need to take.

How long will it take before I start to notice a change?

Oh, if only it were that simple – for example, 'take two action steps before bedtime and call me in the morning if there's no change!' There's no silver bullet with regard to change, I'm afraid. It takes time and patience, and each person's Action Plan will vary depending on his or her situation. My advice at this early stage is not to panic about that now; work out what needs to change first … and then panic (only joking). Seriously, the length of time it takes to make any kind of positive change in your life is immaterial; it's achieving the desired result that counts.

I've read stuff like this before and it hasn't worked for me. What's so different about your book?

I'm unable to answer the first part of this question because only you will know why other approaches haven't 'flicked your switch'. As for what's different about my book, again only you can decide. (I'm biased so I couldn't possibly comment!) But what I *can* tell you is what's the same – you. You're the same person who still wants to make change; you just need to find the right motivation to do so and be ready to step up to the plate and take action. After all, it's not the number of 'tools in the shed' that count, but how and if you use them.

If the book is about burnout, why are we talking about energy management too?

Here's how I see it. I see burnout (or any resulting consequences of excessive or prolonged stress) and effective energy management as being two sides of the same coin; in other words, if you're feeling highly stressed, you're unlikely to be bouncing around like an Easter Bunny all day. I feel there's an interdependent relationship between these two things, which is why, throughout the book, you'll see the two terms used interchangeably (i.e. stress/energy), and why I've taken a two-pronged approach to the topic.

What exactly is burnout?

The concept of burnout isn't a new one, and neither is the idea of effective energy management, but what exactly is burnout?

This is a hard one to answer in some ways, because the term 'burnout' is relatively new, isn't recognized everywhere as a specific condition, and related symptoms tend to come under the broad heading of 'stress'. So am I experiencing stress or am I experiencing burnout? Well, that would depend on whom you are talking to, because what also seems to have added to this general confusion is the fact that since the term emerged, its interpretation has become just as ambiguous. Over the last five years, I've seen it used to describe any number of stress-related disorders, depending on who was using the term and who was listening. For example, it could mean anything from experiencing general everyday stress, to serious work/stress overload or simply having a bad hair day.

However, for the purposes of this book, I'll be using a version that combines the similarities between some common interpretations of burnout, which is, 'The resulting physical and psychological effects of experiencing prolonged or excessive stress'. As Thomas put it, 'For me, burnout felt like I was the little Dutch boy who kept putting his finger in the dike to plug the holes, but the townspeople never came to save me.'

The stress model I'll share with you is based on my own theory about where stress ends and burnout begins, and in Chapter 1 we'll be exploring this close relationship more. But for now, though, let's consider for a moment why burnout appears to be becoming an ever-increasing problem for so many people, regardless of their occupations.

The art of chemical abuse

Developing research in the area of stress and stress management over the last ten years has given us more tools and techniques than we can shake a stick at. Yet, it would appear that despite this wealth of resources, we still have something to learn. It's either that, or we're just not paying attention.

In the western world, we seem to have become conditioned towards treating the symptoms or consequences of poor stress and energy management, rather than addressing the cause itself. As a result, we've dug ourselves into a rut – a permanently fatigued rut that we've come to accept as 'normal'. This is life in the twenty-first century, so we'd better just get used to it.

Having accepted our exhausted fate, many of us have turned our attention to finding creative ways to boost our ever-flagging energy levels and, in doing so, have become masters of the art of chemical abuse. Caffeine, sugar, refined carbs and energy drinks help us to wind up and combat '3 p.m.-itis'; we delude ourselves into thinking that nicotine is helping our stress levels; and then wash it all down with alcohol at night to help us to wind down again.

In short, we've become experts at self-abuse as we hype up our energy levels to keep going way beyond our normal physical and psychological limits. And if it all gets too much, well, we can always reach for the drugs for relief from all those tension headaches, aching backs and bouts of insomnia. Talk about addressing the symptom and not the cause.

Another common side effect of our losing battle in the stress/energy war seems to be an increased vulnerability to the annual visit from a not-so-welcome guest called exhaustion, and its three best friends: colds, flu and viruses. Without fail, every time we take any significant 'down time', one or more of them arrive on our doorstep, bags in hand, for an over-extended stay. This is a fate we appear to have become resigned to, in much the way someone strapped to the back of a runaway horse might be.

Resolutions ...

Having survived the onslaught of our unwelcome guests, we take some time out and, after a while, again start to feel energized, happy and engaged with life again. During this time, as we lie back into the arms of relaxation, another annual event often occurs – the return of the resolution.

Having realized just how completely exhausted we've become, we resolve to do something about it. No more talking, no more thinking – just action. The result is a catalogue of new resolutions about taking more 'time out' for ourselves, eating better, exercising more, not eating lunch at our desks, picking up those hobbies again, and cutting back on all that overtime we've been doing. And we really mean it too ... really we do ... honest. Until, that is, we get back into the swing of that thing called life again and watch our new-found resolutions turn to dust. And so the pattern begins again.

... and their saboteurs

So why does this pattern continue to occur for the majority of us? There can be many reasons, far too many to list in fact, but from experience as a coach, here's a classic 'top 10' of commonly used reasons (or excuses) that I'm sure most of us can identify with:

- We lack the motivation, discipline or commitment to follow through.
- We're simply being unrealistic.
- We find it hard to break old patterns of behaviour, or we fall back into them when we return to our normal routines or when under pressure.
- We don't have the support of our friends, colleagues or family.
- We find it hard to say 'no' to other people and keep taking on more work than we can reasonably handle.
- We think we're being selfish for wanting something for ourselves because we're used to putting everyone else's needs before our own.
- We tell ourselves that we 'don't have time', and make plans to start again 'when it's all over', but never do.
- We're not good at being assertive and standing up for ourselves and our own needs.
- We get cold feet and use stalling tactics like procrastination because it's all starting to look 'too hard'.
- We don't actually believe we can achieve our resolutions.

OK, it's time for some truth. How many of these reasons have you used, or are still using? But don't worry – we've all done it before and I'm sure we'll keep on doing it too. It's called the human condition, and with this condition comes the ability to justify, rationalize and talk ourselves into, or out of, just about anything. It's another art form we've learnt well.

However, if you're reading this book, it is likely that you're ready to take responsibility for your feelings, and to start making some serious changes in your life, so well done you. All you need now is a plan of action that's realistic, a good dose of discipline and commitment, and a healthy sprinkling of time and patience. I can help you with the first part of this equation, but the rest is up to you.

1

Where stress ends and burnout begins

Topic Teasers

- Do you understand the difference between pressure and stress?
- Do you understand the difference between stress and burnout?
- Do you understand the role of your subconscious in the stress equation?
- Are you able to spot the warning signs of excessive stress and energy imbalance?
- Could you be more susceptible to burnout than others?

Stress and the energy equation

Before we start exploring effective energy management, let's dedicate this chapter to understanding the relationship between stress and burnout.

There are many great resources on the topic of stress, its various symptoms, and how to manage them more effectively. Here's a quick recap of what we might already know about stress. For example:

- There's healthy stress that can stimulate us in a positive way and unhealthy stress that doesn't.
- Our perception of a situation will determine how we respond to it.
- Pressure is usually an external event that triggers a 'stress response' in us and can also be self-inflicted too.
- Everyone's ability to cope with stress differs, and can depend on a variety of factors such as life experiences, coping mechanisms, perceptions, beliefs, etc.
- There seem to be two key aspects in the stress equation: how we perceive stress and the length of time we're experiencing it for.
- The symptoms of stress are as wide as they are varied.
- Stress only becomes negative when it begins to exceed our ability to effectively cope with it.
- Although we experience the same stress response to both positive

and negative events, it's the negative ones that are the most disruptive in the long term.

- When we're experiencing stress, we need to find healthy ways of reducing the build-up of stress chemicals in our bodies.

There's a lot of 'obvious' information that we're supposed to know, yet we still keep getting the balance wrong. So, let's remind ourselves again of the basics by taking a quick look at the stress response.

Fight or flight?

We're all familiar with the term 'fight or flight'. This is when we experience a short-term stress reaction to an event; a reaction that enables us to respond quickly to an unexpected or potentially life-threatening event (like last-minute shopping on Christmas Eve or the first day of the sales at the most expensive store in town).

When this happens, we experience a chemical chain reaction that prepares us either to run away or to protect ourselves. Here's a simplified version of what happens.

The pituitary gland kick-starts the process by releasing a hormone called adrenocorticotropic hormone (ACTH), which in turn sends out a bunch of messages to other glands in the body such as the adrenal glands as it calls for reinforcements to come and join the potential battle.

These willing reinforcements arrive in the form of chemicals such as adrenaline (to enhance the speed of our reactions) and cortisol (adrenaline's wing man and back-up supply), both of which help us to fine tune our fighting tactics and responses.

Our nervous system doesn't miss out on the action either as the increased chemical load we're receiving helps us to make a rapid assessment of our situation and to come up with an appropriate course of action.

Once we feel the perceived threat has passed, our hormone levels begin to return to normal, along with our blood pressure, heart rate and metabolism. The threat has passed and all is well with the world again. All in all, the whole experience is usually relatively short-lived.

Janet

I didn't realize I was heading for burnout. It just seemed to finally hit me. Before then I just tried to keep focused and to put all the anger I was feeling behind me. Then an incident happened that cast doubt on my professionalism at work. My anger overwhelmed me; it was the final straw. I walked away and took stress leave.

Prolonged resistance

Research tells us that when we're experiencing periods of long-term or constant pressure in our lives, our body enters what's known as a 'resistance phase' (see Figure 1.1).

When this happens, the normal call for a chemical retreat doesn't occur, and the body continues to pump the required fight or flight chemicals to the battle front.

The resistance phase can last for as long as an individual is able physically and psychologically to resist the stress she is experiencing, or is able to sustain this heightened mode of operation. For some, the threshold may be a few months, while for others it can take a couple of years before exhaustion finally starts to set in.

Factors influencing this time period can include an individual's past experiences, general health, beliefs about yourself and the world and/ or your coping mechanisms. This is why the stress response is such an individual experience for each person.

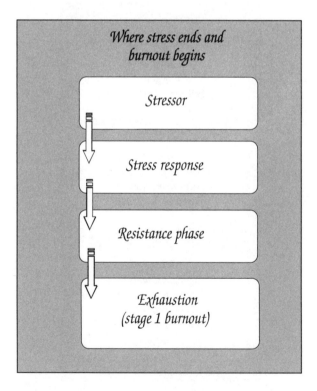

Figure 1.1 Where stress ends and burnout begins

Stages of burnout

Reflecting on my own experience of burnout it was easy to see that there were several stages before I finally hit the wall. My research since confirms this to be the case. So here's a summary of what appear to be the common stages of burnout.

Stage One: Exhaustion

No matter how long we've remained in the resistance stage, eventually our ability to continually resist or cope with the stress we're experiencing will decline. Enter stage left – exhaustion (see Figure 1.2).

Just as our bodies weren't designed to facilitate long periods of physical exertion, we weren't designed to sustain prolonged periods of unrelieved stress either; so without the chance to call off the reinforcements, our body starts to send us subtle warning signs that a system overload is occurring. For example, our sleep cycle can become affected,

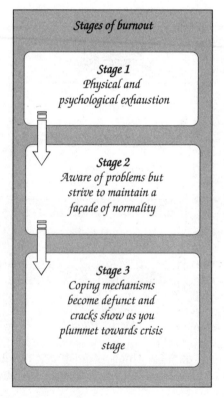

Figure 1.2 Stages of burnout

or we may start to notice a general feeling of lethargy or lingering illnesses that just won't go away.

We may become more irritable than usual, start losing our appetite, or gaining weight. We might become forgetful or start experiencing symptoms of anxiety or depression; muscle tension; headaches or a whole raft of other possible early warning signs.

All these warning signs are your body's way of trying to send you the message that stress overload is occurring and that it's time to slow down, reduce the stress levels, and allow yourself time to recover. However, during this time, we can also seem to suffer from a breakdown in communication, as more often than not we ignore the messages we're receiving and push on with a healthy dose of denial towards Stage Two.

Stage Two: The façade begins – pushing past exhaustion

The length of time that a person takes to reach Stage Two appears to be a variable factor depending on the individual's health, disposition and relationship with stress, and there can be many reasons why we continue to push ourselves past the point of exhaustion. For example, we may be in denial or feel we're still able to 'keep going' regardless of how we're feeling.

Alternatively, we could be suffering from an unhealthy dose of social influence and be more concerned about how our situation might look to others and whether we'll be viewed as a failure or inadequate in some way. Or we may just not see it coming; the human body is amazing in its capacity to put up with no end of abuse before it falls over. We just learn to adapt and keep moving.

Whatever our reasons, as we adopt our 'the show must go on' attitude, we start to experience a new level of intensity in existing physical and psychological symptoms as well as some new and not so good ones too. For example, short-term memory loss, self-imposed isolation, a growing sense of disillusionment and dissatisfaction, a devastating sense of loss and/or sadness, an increasingly negative attitude towards life in general, reduced productivity and morale or an increased insensitivity and harshness towards others (often designed to keep people away so that no one can see the cracks developing in our façade), to name but a few.

For the sake of our overall health, the ideal model would be to move through this phase to Stage Three as quickly as possible, due to the long-term impacts that Stage Two can have on our physical and psychological welfare.

Stage Three: The final stage – crisis or burnout

Stage Three of burnout is when the coping mechanisms that have tried to hold mind, body and soul together during Stage Two finally throw in the towel and call it a day. They've tried to warn us subtly, and then not so subtly, and now they're left with no option but to go on strike.

Symptoms experienced during Stage Two can become accentuated during this time and an individual may start to feel that his or her world is caving in. Even simple routine tasks become challenging, and just making it through the day without falling apart becomes the primary goal.

As emotions flood to the surface, all we want to do is crawl into the hole that we feel is now surrounding us, and not come out again. Questions like 'Who, if anyone, should I tell?' and 'What will people think of me?' race through our minds. Perhaps these questions come from our species' in-built survival instinct to avoid at all costs any signs of what we perceive to be 'weakness'. If we're seen to be vulnerable, we feel we're history. Who knows? But what I do know from my own experience is that when we feel as if we've hit rock bottom, there's only one way to go – and that's up.

Recovery

Recovery – yes, I use the word with complete confidence here because I truly believe that recovery from what can feel like the seven torments of hell is possible, and that further relapses within six months can be prevented. I also believe that it's possible to regain your passion for life, and to be able to experience the odd bad day without panicking that you're heading for burnout again. Yes, I believe that all this is possible. But what's important here is that you do, and that you're ready to make the necessary changes to your life and how you're living it.

James

My experience of burnout has taught me so many lessons. For example, I'm more aware of looking after myself emotionally, work wise, etc. I'm stronger and more assertive now and better at saying 'no' to people. I've radically changed the way I interact with others and have learnt how to get things back on track again quickly if I feel I'm getting stressed again.

From speaking to people over the last two years, I discovered that a common trend among those who experienced burnout again within six months was the fact that no significant changes were made in their lives. They had taken stress leave, but then jumped right back on the same bus they were travelling on before. It all comes back to stepping up to that plate, grabbing this beast by the horns and taking it on, no matter how ugly or hairy it might look. Otherwise we're just living out the much quoted definition for insanity. You know, doing the same thing over and over again and expecting a different result.

Factors influencing how we respond to stress

To finish this chapter, here are some additional factors that can influence the ways that we respond to stress and ultimately affect our susceptibility to burnout. Do any of them look familiar?

- How emotionally attached we feel towards an outcome or goal.
- Maintaining high or unrealistic expectations of ourselves and others.
- How passionate we are about our work (a sad irony is that passionate people who love their work are also at high risk of burnout).
- Tendencies towards perfectionism.
- Lack of flexibility or an inability to adapt quickly to changing circumstances.
- Confusion over what's expected of us, our role and/or responsibilities.
- Taking on more than can be realistically achieved while trying to maintain the status quo.
- Feeling a lack of control over our lives.
- Experiencing continual change.
- Trying to control factors that are outside our scope of control rather than paying attention to how these factors are impacting on us and focusing on what we can influence or control.

OK, so we've explored burnout and its relationship to stress. Now it's time to start moving forward and learning more about our external world and our internal energy reserve.

2

Energy vampires

- Are you able to identify your own energy vampires?
- Are you getting a good return on your energy investment?

Now that we understand more about the relationship between stress and the various stages of burnout, let's take a look at some of the possible impacts this can have on our energy levels and overall ability to feel fully engaged with life. To do this, I'd like to introduce you to the nemesis of effective energy management, but first we will explore the concept of energy itself.

Origins of energy management

When it comes to understanding the origins of our natural energy or 'chi' (life force or vital energy) we can learn a great deal from the ancient philosophies of Traditional Chinese Medicine (TCM).

In TCM, health is all about balance. According to Selby in the book *The Ancient and Healing Art of Chinese Herbalism* (1998), 'keeping fit and healthy is to maintain balance, and illness is viewed as the result of being unbalanced'. She goes on to say that 'it is fundamental to Chinese philosophy that all life is in a state of constant change. This is true as much of the world around us as it is of our own bodies and emotions. Good health can be restored only with balance and harmony. Influenced from both within and without, our body and mind's balance is constantly being upset, leaving us vulnerable to all manner of ailments.'

In acknowledgement of these changing dynamics, TCM works from a perspective of treating the 'whole person' rather than the symptoms alone. These philosophies align closely with the approach of this book; for example:

- An acknowledgement that we operate in an ever-changing environment where our energy continually shifts from balanced to unbalanced and back again.

8

- Exploring the various external and internal factors that can positively or negatively impact on our ability to maintain a natural state of energy balance.
- An acceptance of the fact that the mind–body connection is critical in the energy equation.

Thomas
It wasn't just my work role alone that led to my experience of burnout. But because of my situation at work, I looked for relief in other things, which just brought more and more 'demands' on my time and made it worse.

The energy bank

You might already be running around like the proverbial bluebottle, and an average day may feel like you're trying to dance on a moving carpet. But how do you know if your energy levels are running too low?

If it helps, think about your energy as being similar to money in your bank account. You have some money (energy) in your account. This is your reserve and, depending on your spending habits and outgoings (how you're expending your energy), this could be a lot, a little or nothing at all.

You also have a regular income (energy you receive back or means of topping up your reserve). However, you've also got to make sure that your incomings (energy) can cover your current outgoings (energy expenditure) while leaving a little in reserve for those unexpected items that can crop up from time to time (a crisis or emergency).

Now, some people may be spending (expending energy) more than they're earning (topping up or receiving energy back) and, as a result, they might keep finding themselves in the red as their balance goes overdrawn and they have no reserve (energy) for those unexpected outgoings (crises or emergencies).

You still get warning signs that your reserve is heading for the red zone (stress overload), and depending on your levels of denial, you'll either keep heading for the red zone or you'll pull yourself back into the black (restore the balance and gain some reserve).

Enter the energy vampires

The 'energy vampire' is a visual analogy that I've been using for some years now to describe something, or someone, that has the ability to drain energy from us at an alarming rate.

Recognizing energy vampires

Unlike traditional vampires with their distinctive fangs, anaemic complexion, bloodshot eyes and funky hair, energy vampires can be hard to spot. They come in various forms and can be very cunning in their ability to exist in your life without you even realizing that they're there, bleeding you of your precious energy reserve.

So what forms can energy vampires take?

From an environmental perspective, energy vampires can represent a negative situation or circumstance that, for various reasons, you feel you're unable to leave, such as a work role that no longer satisfies you, a goal that you're no longer motivated to achieve, financial worries, or an unhealthy home environment.

From a social perspective, energy vampires may take the form of friends, family members or work colleagues who demonstrate their mastery at the art of energy extraction through various displays of power games, 'poor me' or victim mentalities, or other controlling or manipulative behaviours.

So what do you do? You can't put a stake through their hearts, sprinkle them with holy water or hang a string of garlic cloves around your neck to protect yourself – unless, that is, you don't want a social life, or like gowns that tie up at the back, or enjoy the idea of solitary confinement for a while!

No, in order to vanquish these vampires, first you need to identify what and who they are, and then you need to create a vampire-free zone. To help you in this task, as a veteran vampire slayer, I've developed a strategy to enable you to do just that. But before we take a look at it, let's take a peek at what an energy vampire attack could look like.

Unleash the misery

Let's take the friend example for a moment. In their defence, these energy vampires often don't know they're vampires, not on a conscious level anyway – and neither do we until we've had an encounter with them, which usually leaves us feeling drained and exhausted. For these energy vampires, energy extraction has just become a learned pattern of behaviour that provides them with a great pay-off – that is, feeling better about themselves. So they continue their behaviour, completely oblivious to the negative impact they're having on people around them.

Characteristics displayed by these energy vampires can include a tendency to lurch from one crisis or drama to another; a 'poor me' or victim mentality; self-sabotaging behaviours; and the fanatical main-tenance of a negative disposition about themselves, other people and life in general. They may often attempt to disguise these tell-tale signs behind a façade of happiness, but once they have you cornered, they unleash a potent and powerful mix of misery on you. This is invisible to the naked eye, but strong and swift in its impact.

Alas, you're doomed

As your energy vampire recounts his or her latest drama, you start to feel listless, your brain begins to ache, and a creeping numbness paralyses you to the spot (much the way a spider will stun its intended victim before immobilizing and eating it). The energy extraction has begun with a schlucking sound that's inaudible to the human ear, and you feel powerless to stop it; this is something that your energy vampire is very aware of. They know you'll feel like a complete fiend if you just say, 'Oh, that's too bad', and beat a hasty retreat; in fact, they're relying on you not doing that – and your genuine desire to help other people.

Before you know it, it's all over. Having gained their emotional pay-off of sympathy, understanding and attention from you, and with their energy levels replenished, they leave you in a sluggish and bewil-dered state as you wonder what on earth hit you. All you can do is watch them skip off into the sunset as they seek out their next unsus-pecting victim. Sound familiar? Indeed yes; been there, experienced it, and have the bite marks to prove it too!

Identifying your energy vampires

From this point forward, I'd like you to think of your own energy vam-pires as those aspects of your life that are having a negative impact on you and your overall sense of well-being. These are the aspects of your life that are creating stress for you and you need to identify them in order to deal with them.

Over the next two chapters we'll be discussing some of the classic energy vampires that can exist in our lives, and you'll be asked to consider which ones may be draining more from your precious energy reserve than they're giving you back. Armed with this knowledge, you'll then explore the intriguing world of your internal energy reserve before putting together your Action Plan.

3

Your external world and internal energy

Topic Teasers

- Did you know that a daily war is being waged over your precious energy reserve?
- How objectively are you able to analyse how and where you're expending your energy?

Let me introduce you to the two opponents in the energy war: your external world and your internal energy reserve.

Opponent one – your external world

Most of us can categorize our external world into two areas – environmental and social (Figure 3.1). Together, these two areas represent the various aspects of our lives – for example, our work, friends, relationships, social life, finances and support networks, and so on.

A relationship exists between these two worlds as they both have the potential to influence, or be influenced by, each other.

They're both well-known feeding grounds for many an energy vampire too, as they provide a plentiful ongoing energy source.

The various factors contained in each of these two worlds will vary from person to person, so you need to identify what your own external world looks like for you. Once you have done this, you'll be able to objectively analyse each factor in terms of the return you're getting on your energy investment.

The lower the return, the more likely it is that this is one of your energy vampires, and the only return you're currently getting is an enhancement to your stress levels.

So let's take a moment to explore your own external world before we look at what your internal energy reserve looks like.

My external world

Create your own model of your external world using Figure 3.2. Don't worry just yet about making an assessment on each of the aspects you

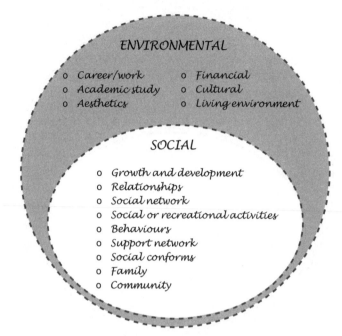

Figure 3.1 Opponent one: your external world

come up with. You'll be doing that in the next two chapters. For now, just think about what makes up your external world for you.

Opponent two – your internal energy reserve

Your internal energy reserve responds and reacts to your external world. I've divided the internal energy reserve into three core energy centres (Figure 3.3):

- physical
- spiritual
- psychological.

All of these lie at the heart of effective stress and energy management.

You continually make withdrawals on your energy reserve (remember the bank account analogy?) as it fuels every aspect of your life and plays a critical role in your sense of well-being, and your ability to manage stress in your life.

Combined, this energy reserve forms the varied aspects of your internal make-up – for example, your physical strength and stamina;

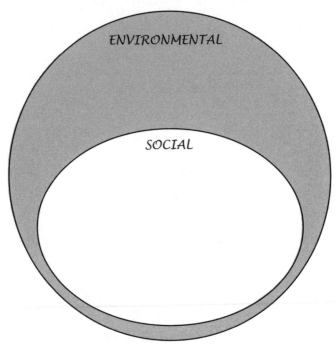

Figure 3.2 My external world

the acquisition and use of knowledge; your emotions, memories, thoughts, beliefs, dreams and ambitions, motivation; and your sense of self-identity.

These three energy centres also maintain a relationship of independence and interdependence within themselves, as well as in terms of how they interact with our external world; because although they exist independently from it, they have the ability to influence, and be influenced by, the state of your external world.

To understand how these relationships work, just think of a time when you felt physically tired. How did you feel at a psychological or emotional level? Did you feel generally fed up or unenthusiastic about life in general? Did everything feel like 'too much trouble', or perhaps you had difficulty in staying focused or became irritable more quickly?

Similarly, if you recently felt down in the dumps about something that had occurred in your external world, did you feel physically lethargic and lacking in energy?

These examples show us the interdependent nature of our external and internal worlds. Rarely is an impact, either positive or negative, experienced in one world without being felt in the other.

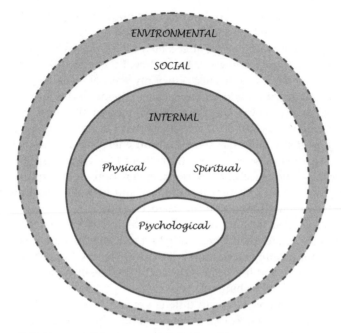

Figure 3.3 Opponent two: your internal energy reserve

When two worlds collide

And so the dance begins, as every day our internal energy reserve inter-acts with our external world, moving from a state of balance to one of unbalance and back again; with each energy transaction influencing how we feel at a physical, psychological and spiritual level.

Margaret
I first noticed I was becoming stressed when I felt unable to cope with my workload and started to worry a lot more than normal. I felt over-whelmed inside and started to become flustered, which isn't something I usually do. After that, things only seemed to get worse.

Under-use versus over-use

There's one more equally damaging and often overlooked opponent in the energy battle that we need to keep an eye out for too. This oppo-nent comes in the form of the under-utilization of your energy reserve, which needs to be monitored just as much as over-use does. Let me use myself as an example to explain what I mean.

I'm a fairly active person. I have a busy life, but with a healthy dose of down time when I need to recharge my batteries. One of the recharge techniques that works for me after a busy phase of activity is just to sit still and watch the world go by for a while. I don't do this because I'm exhausted or depressed. It's just one of my ways of recharging.

However, my threshold for being able to maintain this form of 'cave time' is usually only around one or two days at the most. At some time during the second day I've noticed that I'm starting to get a little fidgety, as if my body has some built-up energy that it needs to get rid of. This makes sense if you think about it. Having topped up my physical, psychological and emotional energy centres, my body is ready to go again, while I've kept it stationary and immobile. So I need to release the build-up to regain the balance again.

Now can you imagine how I'd start to feel if I forced myself to stay put for longer than I needed to? I'd probably become even more fidgety, and possibly more than a little irritable too. I might also start to feel isolated, and my sleep cycle might become disrupted due to all the excess energy I've built up.

Because we all operate with different energy levels, we all have different energy thresholds too. What constitutes balance for me may be very different from someone else. This is why, once we have learned ways to manage our stress effectively, and to restore our energy balance, we need to make sure we monitor under-utilization of energy as much as over-use. Either of these can upset the balance.

So now let's take stock of your external world, and your hidden (or not so hidden) energy vampires – otherwise known as an energy-sucking source of stress.

4

External world: assessing your environment

Topic Teasers

- Is your career/work giving you a great return on your energy investment or is it making nothing but hefty withdrawals?
- If you're currently studying, have you taken into account the impact that this may be having on your available energy reserve?
- Are the aesthetics of your environment energizing you and in what way?
- Is your living environment having a positive or negative impact on your energy reserve?
- How is your current financial situation affecting how and where you invest your energy?
- Is your energy balance being influenced by cultural norms?

Have you ever felt you're putting in more energy than you get out of a situation? If so, you might benefit from knowing how to maximize that precious resource, your energy. This chapter looks at how well you're rewarded for the amount of energy you are investing. To measure it, I use the ROEI scale – ROEI stands for 'Return on Energy Investment'.

The ROEI scale

I've separated the two areas of our external world into two chapters. In this one, we explore some of the possible factors that may exist in your environmental world, and in the following chapter we'll be exploring your social world.

You'll be asked to make an assessment of how you feel about the different aspects of your external world with the use of questions (Energy Pulse Checks), and the Return on Energy Invested (ROEI) scale (as shown in Table 4.1) with a rating box that looks like the one shown below:

Energy Investment Area	ROEI Rating
Current work role	

The ROEI scale has three ratings:
1 = little or no ROEI
2 = moderate ROEI
3 = above average or maximum ROEI
Let's explore how you might be feeling for each of these ratings.

Table 4.1 The ROEI scale

Example	ROEI Rating
Little or no ROEI: You're investing a large amount of energy in this area, but are receiving little or no return from your investment. This area of your life may be a significant cause of stress for you and often leaves you feeling drained, unhappy, frustrated, disappointed, disillusioned, etc.	1
Moderate ROEI: You're investing a great deal of energy in this area of your life, but feel you're receiving only a moderate return on your investment. The balance between the stress this area creates for you and the energy you get back from it may differ from day to day, with little or no consistency. Some days feel harder than others, and you're grateful for any good days that come along. You may experience some of the same negative emotional responses to this aspect of your life as you would for a little or no ROEI.	2
Above average or maximum ROEI: This area of your life is providing you with a consistently high return on the energy you're investing in it. You experience little or no stress here and usually feel energized, inspired, motivated or 'in the zone' when you're around this area of your life as it provides you with a constant feel-good factor.	3

Now let's take a more detailed look at your external world.

Career or work role

We spend an inordinately large amount of time at work and sometimes we may underestimate the important role it plays in our lives. Work helps us to define and understand who we are and what we're capable of; it inspires and motivates us; it helps us to identify our role in the world; and it meets our intrinsic need to feel a connection to something bigger than ourselves.

Common career traps

However, two common career traps we can experience are:

The rut and bob manoeuvre

This means we get stuck in a rut. Or, alternatively, we engage in aimless 'bobbing' from one job role to another with no clear direction or plan of where we're going or why.

The tunnel shuffle

This is when the only career path we're able to see in front of us is the same as the one we've already travelled. When we get caught in this career trap, we can end up staying on a career path long after its expiry date, and long after it has ceased to inspire or motivate us.

Once we've been in either of these situations for a while, we may start to feel as if we're just going through the motions. We may begin to feel stressed, unhappy, frustrated, bored, demotivated, unproductive and generally dead from the neck up. The mere effort of going to work and getting through the day exhausts us. If this sounds familiar, then welcome to one of your energy vampires.

Unless we become angry or inspired enough to take action, we can remain in this situation for some time, as we abandon our career aspirations with the same resigned inevitability we may have developed towards that unwelcome annual holiday guest or to being strapped to the back of our runaway horse. However, this time, our runaway horse has dropped dead from lack of interest.

Career or work role ROEI: above average or maximum

So what might an above average or maximum career ROEI look like? Well, it might provide us with:

- opportunities to work in areas we're passionate about or that energize us;
- a sense of connection to something bigger than ourselves;
- a strong alignment between our personal and professional values;
- opportunities to channel our natural strengths, talents and abilities;
- feelings of high motivation, of feeling inspired or 'being in the zone';
- a lingering sense of excitement;
- a work day that doesn't feel like work at all.

When we're happy at work, it can actually feed or top up our energy reserve as we gain the same, or more, back from our energy investment.

How many of these career energizers are you currently experiencing? And if you used to feel them but now don't, what has changed for you?

Career or work role ROEI: little or none

Now let's look through the mirror the other way and explore what a low career ROEI might look like. For example, it might leave us feeling like we're:

- under-valued and/or under-utilized;
- 'stuck in a rut' or lacking direction;
- bored, frustrated or dissatisfied;
- no longer growing professionally and/or personally;
- exhausted, lethargic and uninspired;
- claustrophobic, trapped or as if we've reached a dead end;
- no longer able to control what's happening around us;
- losing our self-confidence and/or self-esteem;
- dead from the neck up.

If your work represents one of your energy vampires, don't underestimate the impact this may be having on you, and your stress levels. An unfulfilling career has a profound ability to suck the life out of you, leaving you feeling drained physically, psychologically and spiritually.

Now it's time to do your own career ROEI assessment.

My career or work role ROEI assessment

Your ROEI assessment should be used purely as a guide to help you prioritize your Action Plan later in the book. There is no complicated or scientific approach to completing your assessment; just use your judgement and some common sense.

For example, if you could identify with most of the bullet points listed under the above average or maximum career ROEI box, then you may decide to rate your career ROEI as a '3'. But if you identified more with the bullet points under the little or no career ROEI, then you may consider rating this area of your external world as a '1'. If, however, you had an even spread across both of these areas, then you may decide to rate your career ROEI as a '2' and target the specific issues you're currently unhappy with as part of your Action Plan.

1 = little or no ROEI
2 = moderate ROEI
3 = above average or maximum ROEI

Energy Investment Area	ROEI Rating
Career/work role	

Regardless of what stage you're currently at in terms of your career, doing a periodic appraisal of the ROEI you're receiving from your work is always a good idea. This way, you'll be continually reinvesting your precious energy where it's needed most.

Academic study

Academic study is another area of our life that can either enhance our energy reserves or our stress levels, depending on when and how we're completing our study, whether we're sufficiently motivated to do so, and the time available.

If you have academic study as part of your environmental world, all these dynamics will have a significant impact on how you're currently feeling about your study demands; to assist you in assessing this area of your life, here's some simple 'yes' or 'no' questions for you to consider:

Academic study: Energy Pulse Check

	Yes	No
Do your study demands leave you feeling drained?	☐	☐
Does your study activity leave you feeling energized/excited?	☐	☐
Do you feel motivated to complete your study?	☐	☐
Do you have allocated study time without distractions?	☐	☐
Is your study tied to your work role?	☐	☐
Are you happy in your work role?	☐	☐
Is your study still applicable to your professional goals?	☐	☐
Do you incorporate 'recharge' times following/between study periods?	☐	☐
Do you feel your current approach to study is successful?	☐	☐
Are you sufficiently motivated to continue with your studies?	☐	☐

My academic study ROEI assessment

If you have academic study down as one of the aspects of your external world, now is the time to make your ROEI assessment. Follow the same approach as before, but use the number of your 'yes' or 'no' answers as your guide this time.

1 = little or no ROEI
2 = moderate ROEI
3 = above average or maximum ROEI

Energy Investment Area	ROEI Rating
Academic study	

Aesthetics and living environment

Aesthetics is another interesting aspect of your external world which is closely linked to your living environment. In this section, we're focusing our attention on your home environment more than your work one (although feel free to consider this aspect too if it's an issue for you).

Aesthetics

Some people could live in a cardboard box and still feel happy. Others need certain aesthetics around them before they feel completely relaxed, comfortable or energized. These might include, for example, water near their home; certain colour schemes; a home facing a certain direction; certain styles of furniture or floor coverings; lots of natural light or wide open spaces.

I'm one of these people. I know this about myself and I ensure, no matter where I am, that I create the right kind of environment around me to assist me in topping up or recharging my energy levels every day.

If we're unhappy with the aesthetics of our living environment, then without realizing it we can start to experience the signs of stress and reduce our ability to effectively recharge our energy levels.

Living environment

For some, this represents their nest or cave, a bolt-hole or sanctuary from the worries, stresses and insanities of the day. It feels secure, comfortable, energizing and loving. For others, it's a place of wonderful mayhem that brings together all the various people and activities that represent their family life. And for others again, their home represents nothing more than a place to crash, lay their head or doss, and it has little or no emotional attachment for them beyond the pain they feel each month when they pay their rent or mortgage!

While our living environments represent different things to each of us, when we're unhappy in them, rather than finding them a safe harbour in a chaotic world, we can find them nothing more than a continued drain on our energy reserve.

Our living environment is also a great example of the interdependence that can exist between the environmental and social aspects of our external world. For example, we may have created a wonderful living environment with all the aesthetic beauty we need to feel relaxed, calm and comfortable, but if our home relationships are unhappy, we can start to view our home environment with less enthusiasm than we would if we felt we were part of a caring and loving relationship.

Similarly, if we're unhappy with our living conditions, we'll only be able to keep our mutual passion alive for so long before simmering frustrations start to take their toll on our relationship.

Aesthetics and living environment: Energy Pulse Check

So how would you rate your current living environment and its aesthetics? Consider the following questions and write your answers in the spaces below each question.

Do you look forward to returning home at the end of the day?

If not, which aspects of your home environment deplete your energy levels?

If yes, which aspects re-energize you?

Do you have somewhere in your home that is dedicated purely to energy renewal?

How important are the aesthetics of your environment to you?

Which aesthetics do you find energizing and uplifting to be around (water, plants, certain colours, etc.)?

How do the current aesthetics of your home make you feel?

What do you feel is missing (if anything)?

Are you able to change the aesthetics at home?

If yes, which aspect(s), if changed, would make the biggest difference to you right now, and when would you be able to complete these changes?

If no, what other options could you explore?

My aesthetics and living environment ROEI assessment

So, if you have aesthetics and/or living environment down as one or two important aspects of your external world, it's time to make your ROEI assessment.

Based on your responses to the previous questions, make your ROEI assessment first of all on the aesthetics of your living environment and then on the living environment itself.

Aesthetics:

1 = little or no ROEI
2 = moderate ROEI
3 = above average or maximum ROEI

Energy Investment Area	ROEI Rating
Home aesthetics	

Living environment:

1 = little or no ROEI
2 = moderate ROEI
3 = above average or maximum ROEI

Energy Investment Area	ROEI Rating
Living environment	

Finances

I'm no financial guru. In fact, it's safe to say that I find accounting as exciting as a poke in the eye. But you don't have to be an expert to understand the positive impact of being in a comfortable debt-free financial state, as compared to the opposite.

If you do feel that your finances could do with an overhaul, and you're at a loss as to how to proceed, then do seek financial expertise or advice as soon as possible. There are numerous great resources to help you and many of them are free.

Even if it's more serious and you feel that your financial circumstances are so entangled that they're beyond help, or that you have no way out of your financial predicament, remember that even a modest plan of action is better than no action at all. It's when we go into denial and try to ignore our financial concerns that we're actually creating a bigger energy drain for ourselves, because our concerns won't go away, and neither will the problem. They'll just lie there and fester until they're addressed. So look your financial demons squarely in the eyes and face them head on. You'll feel much better for it in the long run, I promise.

Finances: Energy Pulse Check

These are the only questions I'm going to address here. If you'd like to take a deeper look at your financial concerns or issues, do seek professional advice.

What are your greatest financial concerns at this stage?

How do your financial circumstances make you feel?

How would you like to feel?

Would you consider this area of your external world as a significant source of stress for you?

If you used to feel more positive about your finances, but now don't, what has changed?

What professional advice have you access to, or could you seek out?

What is stopping you from seeking professional advice?

What is one action that you could take today that would make the greatest impact on your current financial situation?

If you're unable to make any changes now, when will you be able to?

My finances ROEI assessment

So, if you have finance down as an important aspect of your external world, now's the time to make your ROEI assessment. Having considered the questions and your current financial circumstances, how would you rate this aspect of your external world?

1 = little or no ROEI
2 = moderate ROEI
3 = above average or maximum ROEI

Energy Investment Area	ROEI Rating
Finances	

Culture

Culture is an interesting and large topic, with many dimensions. For the purposes of this book, I'm using the word 'culture' to refer to established expectations; in other words, what are considered to be accepted behaviours or boundaries to do with how we 'should' or 'should not' behave and interact with one another.

These cultural norms surround us every day, within our homes, our workplace, our society and in the country we live in; but for this exercise, we're going to narrow our focus down to just three areas:

- our home culture
- our workplace culture
- our immediate 'clan' or 'tribe' culture (our family, friends, work colleagues, etc.).

Our home culture

Everyone's home dynamic is different, but one thing that remains the same is the way in which we establish certain ground rules about how we 'should' or 'shouldn't' behave towards one another. We do this by establishing expectations and boundaries – a code of conduct if you like.

Our workplace culture

All organizations have a culture, an accepted or role-modelled way of behaving in the workplace, and this will either enhance or detract from an organization's ability to achieve its strategic and operational goals, or to inspire and retain its people.

Organizational cultures can be consistent across an organization or fragmented, with small 'subcultures' being formed, depending on the size and geographical spread of the organization.

Over the last ten years or so, this area of workplace efficiency has become increasingly important, and more and more organizations are becoming proactive in the establishment of their expectations around how they want their people to interact, communicate and work together. Some organizations have even linked these areas of behavioural development into their training and performance-management systems.

If we are happy with the culture of our workplace, we can find the environment uplifting and energizing. If, however, we are at odds with this culture, we can become extremely stressed as we expend huge amounts of energy either trying to fight the cultural norms or trying to adapt to them.

Our immediate 'clan' or 'tribe' culture

A long time ago, our caveman ancestors lived in tribes as a way of increasing their chances of survival. They hunted, gathered and prepared food as a group, protected one another from harm, and created the next generation of little cavepeople together. Although the emphasis on survival of the species has now lessened, we do still live in similar tribal environments.

Our new tribe or clan is made up of our immediate family, friends, work colleagues, peers, managers, role models and mentors, and so on – basically, anyone who has the ability to influence how we feel and how we behave. We may go to our tribe for advice, to seek approval and support, or for guidance and direction, and as such these people can play a critical role in our lives.

Some clans or tribes are supportive and nurturing, providing us with new insights and perspectives, while allowing us the space and freedom to define our own behaviours and actions in a way that feels right for us. But other clans or tribes can be less supportive, as we feel the need to seek their approval or to conform in some way with little consideration for our own needs.

The extent to which we allow ourselves to be influenced or directed by the thoughts, beliefs, rules and demands of others, or the level to which we feel we need to seek their approval before taking action, will determine how much internal conflict (and therefore stress) we experience, or how much energy we gain.

Culture: Energy Pulse Check

Consider the following questions for each of these three cultural dimensions.

Our home culture
How would you describe the culture of your home environment?

How does it make you feel?

Are you aware of the accepted cultural norms of your home environment?

Does this environment enhance or deplete your energy levels (and therefore raise your stress levels)?

In which way does it energize you?

In which way does it deplete your energy levels and raise your stress levels?

How long has it been like this for you?

If your cultural environment used to energize you but is now depleting you, what has changed?

Are you able to influence this environment and, if so, in what way?

Our workplace culture
Are you aware of accepted cultural norms of your organization and/or immediate work environment?

How would you describe this cultural environment?

Do the accepted behaviours of your organization differ from the accepted behaviours of your immediate work environment?

If so, in what ways?

Does this environment enhance or deplete your energy levels?

In what way does it energize you?

In what way does it deplete your energy levels and raise your stress levels?

How long has it been like this for you?

If the cultural environment of your workplace used to energize you but is now depleting you, what has changed?

Are you able to influence the culture of your immediate work environment and, if so, in what way?

What change could you make today that would make the biggest difference to you at this time?

Our immediate clan or tribe culture
Who belongs to your immediate clan/tribe? (You may want to break them up into immediate family, friends, work colleagues, mentors, etc.).

If asked to assess each member of your clan/tribe in terms of their positive or negative influence on you and your stress and energy levels, how would you rate each member (e.g. you could use a 'tick' for positive impact and a cross for a negative impact to keep it nice and simple)?

What do your ratings tell you about your clan/tribe?

What role does your clan/tribe play in your life (list the various roles if you have more than one group listed in the first question in this section)?

How much do you feel your own behaviour or actions are influenced by your clan/tribe and in what way?

Has it always been this way for you? And, if not, what has changed and why?

What do you think this information tells you about yourself?

What would need to change for you to feel less influenced by your clan/tribe?

What benefits are there for you in keeping any existing negative influencers as part of your clan/tribe?

In an ideal world, what would your tribe look like and what role would these people play in your life?

What would need to happen to create this ideal scenario?

My culture ROEI assessment

So, if anything culturally based appears in your external world, now's the time to make your ROEI assessment(s).

1 = little or no ROEI
2 = moderate ROEI
3 = above average or maximum ROEI

Energy Investment Area	ROEI Rating
Home	
Immediate workplace	
Organizational (if different)	
My clan/tribe	

Well done. You've made it through the first round of self-assessments. And this brings us to the end of the environmental component of your external world. I hope you've found this exercise useful and that it has given you some food for thought along the way too.

OK, take a well-earned break, have a cup of tea, a snooze or whatever takes your fancy, and then come back to complete the final element of your external world: the social dynamic.

5

External world: assessing your social environment

Topic Teasers

- When was the last time you experienced a growth 'spurt'?
- Do you find your intimate relationships energizing or energy depleting?
- Have you surrounded yourself with energy vampires?
- Are you engaging in behaviour that could be depleting your energy reserves?
- Do you let other people's behaviour get to you?
- How much energy are you expending just trying to 'fit in'?
- What role is your family playing in the energy equation?

Exploring social factors

In the context of this model, the social factors of your external world represent those aspects of your life that have the potential to influence how you define yourself, your role in life, or as part of your immediate clan/tribe.

As you move through this chapter, use the same process to assess each topic covered as you did before.

Personal and professional growth and development

As a species, we're genetically disposed to evolve, grow and develop; our knuckle-dragging descendants have been doing it since they first learnt how to stand upright on two legs. We also seem to have an innate drive to reach for new limits and, as we push back these boundaries, we learn more about ourselves, our environment and what we're capable of.

When we deny or ignore this in-built drive to continually evolve, I feel we start to wither, and may become only shadows of the person we could potentially be. This self-imposed ceiling on our development can also signal that at some level we've decided to settle for what we feel we may deserve, rather than what we truly desire or what we're actually capable of.

Personal growth: becoming the observer

Personal growth can take many forms. We can grow through life experience and the lessons we learn; by enrolling on a course; or through regular interactions with a coach or mentor.

Another form of personal growth can come from just becoming an observer in our own lives. Let me explain what I mean. Every experience we have, whether positive or negative, presents us with an opportunity to learn something new about ourselves and how we interact with the world around us. We play the role of observer in the lives of those around us every day, as we watch other people's behaviours and emotions: what they say and do; who they do it with; when and why. We then use these observations to form views about those people.

Becoming the observer in our own lives means developing the ability to step periodically outside our own experiences, and to detach from them emotionally for long enough to consider the impact of our own behaviour, emotions or feelings on ourselves and others, just as we would if we were observing someone else.

When we do this, we create opportunities to ask ourselves questions – something we may not do that often. For example:

- Why do I feel like this?
- Why did I behave in that way?
- Why was that so important to me?
- Why do I want to do this?
- How did my behaviour impact on the other person/situation?
- Was that what I wanted to achieve? If not, how could I have handled it differently?
- What was driving my behaviour, or where is it coming from?
- What assumptions am I making here? Am I basing my viewpoint on fact or perception?
- What do I really believe about this situation/person/myself?
- What am I not really dealing with here or what could I be trying to avoid?
- What does that tell me about myself?

When you first begin this form of self-reflection, you'll probably use it more in a post-event way, as you think back over your day. But as you become more practised at it, you'll be able to use it more proactively by applying it to future events as a way of running through various scenarios before they arise, to ensure your behaviour is in line with the outcome you want.

Professional development: avoiding the traps

Professional development is a beautiful thing, but it can also hold some common traps for us if we're not careful. Traps such as enrolling on a course without any clear objective, or the trap of doing training for the sake of being seen to do something, or because it provides us with nothing more than a diversion from the tedious routine of our lives.

Another common trap can be ineffective planning regarding the level of energy and commitment required to complete a project, or being unrealistic about our ability to balance our new learning curve against other commitments in our lives.

As an energy enhancer, we've all experienced the feeling of elation when we overcome a learning obstacle or barrier, achieve a new level of understanding, or develop a new skill. It boosts our confidence and gives us a great buzz. But when our growth and development is too demanding, unrealistic or non-existent, we can start to suffer the opposite effect; and this is when it starts to get messy, as our potential great experience starts to feel more like a pressure, a routine, or just 'another thing we have to do'. And as a result, we start to feel stressed, drained, flat, lethargic, uninspired or unmotivated, which I'm guessing was not the aim of the game when you set off down that road.

So if your growth and development are important aspects of your social world, consider the following questions and then complete your assessment of where things are at for you at this time.

Personal growth and development: Energy Pulse Check

When was the last time you felt you experienced a personal growth spurt and what was it?

If it's been a while, what has changed for you?

When was the last time you took a step outside your personal comfort zone and how did it feel?

How (if at all) did this experience influence your viewpoint of 'zone jumping' in the future?

If your experience of zone jumping was a negative one, then if presented with the same oportunity again, what would you do differently?

If your experience was a positive one, what did you learn about yourself?

Do you ever view negative experiences in your life as positive growth opportunities?

Do you ever use self-reflection as a way of developing yourself?

Do the members of your clan/tribe support you in your personal development?

How might this have been influencing you, or still be influencing you?

Professional growth and development: Energy Pulse Check

When was the last time you felt you experienced a professional growth spurt and what was it?

When was the last time you took a step outside your professional comfort zone at work and how did it feel?

What happened when you did this?

How did this experience influence your viewpoint of 'zone jumping' in the future at work?

Do you ever view negative work experiences as positive growth opportunities?

What professional training/development have you undertaken in the last year?

Were these experiences energizing or otherwise in their impact on your stress/energy levels?

My personal and professional growth and development ROEI assessment

Having considered the questions for both personal and professional development, how would you now rate these two aspects?

1 = little or no ROEI
2 = moderate ROEI
3 = above average or maximum ROEI

Energy Investment Area	ROEI Rating
Personal growth and development	
Professional growth and development	

Relationships

The topic of intimate relationships with 'significant others' is a book in itself, and we're all familiar with relationships past and present that have either made us feel great, or have brought us more heartache than they were worth.

We'll be exploring your relationships with your friends and family in the next section, so for now let's focus on your current intimate relationship with your husband, wife or life partner.

Note:
If you're currently single, why not use this section to think about what your ideal partner would be like, and what kind of person they would be attracted to. You may find some additional areas for personal development floating to the surface that will help you to attract your dream partner. I've also included some Energy Pulse Check questions for single people at the end of this section.

Basic instincts

We all know that at a very basic level, our natural instinct to find the 'perfect partner' is largely driven by an inherited desire to maintain the survival of the species. However, as a species, we seem to have evolved the art of mate-matching to a whole new level. As we seek out our hearts' desires, we're looking for an emotional experience that can be fulfilled by few other areas of our lives, and a level of intimacy with another human being that fills our hearts with love and passion. We want to feel safe, loved and secure.

Apart from achieving this universally sought-after and desired emotional state, we also seem to bring our own motivators for wanting to find our perfect match into the equation; and it's these motivators, whether you had realized it or not, that will often determine the match you end up with. Let me expand on this observation.

For some people, finding a life partner is also about finding someone who can 'fill a gap' or 'complete' them in some way. For them, being single is not a happy place. They see singledom as saying nothing more to the world and themselves than 'I am undesirable, unlovable and unworthy', and having a special someone in their lives triggers a reversal of this emotional state for them.

A sad irony of this approach, however, can be that the search for love is often continually blighted by unsuitable matches, as one failed relationship after another only serves to confirm a person's original beliefs about him or herself (i.e. 'I am undesirable, unlovable and unworthy'; it's like a form of self-inflicted, self-fulfilling prophecy).

So, other than trying to depress you, why am I mentioning this? This is why. If you've found yourself in one disastrous relationship after another, and you're beginning to despair of ever finding your one true love, perhaps it's time to take a step back from the whole process for a moment and ask yourself the following questions:

- What exactly am I looking for in my life partner?
- What kind of person would I need to be in order to attract this person? OR: What kind of person would someone like that be attracted to?
- Am I that person? (Be brutally honest with yourself here.)
- What do I need to develop/change to become that person?

Talking to single men and women over the years, I often ask them what they're looking for in a life partner, and most are able to roll off a list of physical characteristics and personality traits relatively easily. But how often do we consider what kind of person someone like that would be attracted to?

It's the old 'like attracts like' principle in action here. After all, someone who is confident, intelligent, a great communicator, happy, thoughtful and kind is unlikely to be attracted to a gloomy person who is low in confidence and self-esteem, self-obsessed and couldn't hold a good conversation if his or her life depended on it! See where I'm going with this?

The same principle can be applied to unhealthy relationships. For example, a controlling and manipulative relationship requires two parties in order to create such an environment – someone to do the controlling or manipulating, and someone to be controlled or manipulated. These parties may exchange roles, or one person may adopt and remain in a specific role, but the same principle applies – like usually attracts like.

When we ask these types of questions, we start taking more responsibility for our role, either in achieving a great relationship, or in continuing to remain in an unhealthy one. If the people closest to us in our lives are truly a reflection of who we are, then what is your current partnership telling you about yourself? This is a hard question to ask yourself I know, but it is worth the effort in the long run.

So, if relationships featured in the social aspect of your external world, take a look at the questions that follow, and then complete your ROEI assessment at the end.

Relationship: Energy Pulse Check (for those who currently have a partner)

How would you describe your current relationship?

How does your current relationship make you feel? (What emotional states do you experience on a consistent basis?)

If you're happy in your relationship, how do you think these feelings are influencing other areas of your life (work, personal growth, etc.)?

If you're unhappy in your relationship, how do you think these feelings might be negatively influencing other areas of your life?

What changes have you noticed in yourself since this relationship came into your life (both positive and negative)?

If you're unhappy in your relationship but you used to be happy, what changed for you?

How do you want to feel about your relationship?

What would need to happen for you to make a change in this area of your life?

What does your relationship provide you with? (What need(s)/role does it meet/play for you?)

What need(s)/role would you like your relationship to play in your life (if different to the above question)?

If you didn't have this current relationship in your life, how do you think you would feel?

What do you think this relationship is telling you about yourself?

Relationship: Energy Pulse Check (for those currently single)

How do you feel about being single?

Do you feel being single is a reflection on who you are as a person? And if so, in what way?

What role do you want a relationship to play in your life?

Describe what you feel would be your perfect match.

What kind of person do you think someone like this would be attracted to?

Do these characteristics describe you?

What do your answers tell you about yourself?

My relationship ROEI assessment

Whether you're in a relationship or currently single, having completed the questions, it's now time to make your ROEI assessment.

1 = little or no ROEI
2 = moderate ROEI
3 = above average or maximum ROEI

Energy Investment Area	ROEI Rating
Relationship	

Social and support network

These two aspects represent our friends and acquaintances (social network) and the extent to which those friends and acquaintances provide us with support during challenging times (support network). Family is covered in a separate section later in this chapter.

It has been proven through numerous studies over the years that people are happier when they have a good social network of friends and those they can call on in times of need. Such people provide us with love and support when we need it and give us a sense of connection to others. This sense of connection energizes us, and these people, unlike our energy vampires, willingly give us their energy when we need it, and we willingly reciprocate this behaviour, no questions asked.

However, thinking back to our original energy vampire example in Chapter 2, this is also where some of our vampires can be lurking, moving quietly around with stealthy movements in the shadows, as they wait for the appropriate time to pounce and drain us of our precious energy reserves.

This is when we need to become assertive to break this cycle of behaviour and to either help them to help themselves, or send them packing and on to a new feeding ground. Think of it as spring cleaning your social network instead of your house.

We'll be discussing some of the tactics and strategies for vanquishing energy vampires in our social network later in Chapter 8, but for now let us consider the following Energy Pulse Check questions.

Social network: Energy Pulse Check

Which members of your social network energize you?

What common characteristics do these people have?

How do you think you could attract more people like this into your life?

Which members of your social network drain you of energy or cause you stress?

What common characteristics do these people have?

How long have these energy vampires been in your life?

Were you aware of their role as energy vampires in your life before now?

Do you want to keep these people in your life and, if yes, why? (What do you gain from having them around?)

If you don't want to keep these people in your life, how can you reduce your contact with them?

Support network: Energy Pulse Check

Do you feel you have a strong support network in your life?

What role does your support network play in your life?

Do you feel comfortable/willing to approach your support network in times of need?

What support do you provide in return to your support network?

If you would like to improve your support network, what steps could you take to do this?

My social and support network ROEI assessment

OK, you're doing very well, so keep up the good work. Now it's time to consider your ROEI for your social network and your support network if either or both of these aspects featured in your external world.

1 = little or no ROEI
2 = moderate ROEI
3 = above average or maximum ROEI

Energy Investment Area	ROEI Rating
Social network	
Support network	

Social and recreational activities

There are times when we all need to let our hair down, let off steam, and generally relax. Hobbies or recreational activities can help us to have fun, release our creativity, express ourselves and unwind, and in some cases they also energize us. In short, they help us to express new dimensions of who we are, so they play a valuable role in the stress/energy balance equation.

This is probably one of the few areas of our lives that operates completely from a win-win perspective, as we rarely engage in a hobby of any kind without a positive 'what's in it for me?' factor being involved.

So, if you already have some extracurricular activities that are providing you with an 'energy top up', that's great; and if you don't, then you may want to consider bringing more of this valuable 'me time' into your life.

Remember, you can't give 100 per cent of yourself to someone else unless you're giving 100 per cent to yourself first. It's a bit like the emergency procedures on a plane that ask you to make sure your own mask is fitted before assisting others. So, taking a little 'me time' to pursue your own interests and hobbies, or to just relax in your own space for a while, isn't about being selfish, it's about being considerate to those you love.

Social and recreational activities: Energy Pulse Check

What hobbies or recreational activities do you like to do?

How do you feel when you're doing these activities?

What needs do they meet for you? OR: How often do you use these activities to 'top up' your energy reserves?

How often do these activities feature in your life?

If you used to do more in this area, what has changed?

Do you find yourself feeling guilty for wanting some time for yourself?

What do you need to change about yourself/your thought processes to overcome these feelings of guilt?

If you don't currently have many hobbies/recreational activities, what activities could you start to introduce?

What needs would these activities meet for you? OR: How will they assist you in topping up your energy reserve?

What steps can you take to make sure these new activities remain in your life?

My social and recreational activities ROEI assessment

Now it's time to rate this aspect of your external world ... by now, you know what to do!

1 = little or no ROEI
2 = moderate ROEI
3 = above average or maximum ROEI

Energy Investment Area	ROEI Rating
Social or recreational activities	

Behaviour (our own and other people's)

Behaviour, like many of the other aspects of our external world, could become a book in itself due to the wide scope of the topic. So I'm going to narrow down our area of focus a little.

When I'm thinking about the potential of behaviour (our own and other people's) to impact on our stress/energy levels, I'll be covering it from two perspectives:

- How our own behaviour can affect our stress/energy levels.
- How our reactions to other people's behaviour can affect our stress/energy levels.

These two perspectives might sound like strange bedfellows but, believe me, we can be our own worst enemy when it comes to creating stress for ourselves from the inside out. So, let's continue to gain some insights into the origins of our own behaviour.

Lights ... and action

Our behaviours are the outcome of a cycle that begins in our subconscious and ends with a result. To get to that end result, it might help for a moment to think of your brain as a video camera with a dual function:

Function 1 is to record all new experiences as they come along and to attach the associated emotions and feelings you experienced at the time to that memory.

Function 2 is to access existing memories of similar experiences to assist you in interpreting each new experience.

This dual process helps us to make sense of the world around us and to make assessments and decisions about what to do next, which is great. However, it can also mean that we're often flying around on automatic pilot, as we continually make decisions today, based only on our experiences of the past.

This can be a good thing when those experiences have been positive ones, but we also need to consider the influence that our negative past experiences may still be having on us today, as we continue to access the same file over and over again without pressing the pause button and questioning what's happening.

The editing room

As we go about our busy lives, we're continually making these video films in our head. Some will become part of our internal film collection (stored memories), and some will never make it out of the editing room alive. This is due to the amount of information being thrown at us on any given day and what we decide is worth holding on to for future reference, and what we decide to discard as irrelevant. After all, there's just so much choice out there; a drama in the workplace, a comedy over lunch, or a romance in the evening. So we decide what we want to hold on to and what we want to let go of by using our in-built editing system.

Here's my non-scientific version of what happens. Our editing system contains all our beliefs, motivators, perceptions, values and expectations – basically, all the stuff that makes us tick – and it all lies beneath the surface in our subconscious. It's the cumulative result of our life experience and it directs how we think, feel and behave, the actions we take, and ultimately the results we achieve in life.

Each result we achieve as a consequence of this cycle will either reinforce an existing belief, motivator, etc., or challenge it by presenting us with an alternative view of the world or ourselves. We then make the decision as to whether to accept this new perspective or belief, and ultimately create a new cycle of emotions, behaviours and actions, or whether to ignore it and let it go. Either way, the end result will continue to feed back into the cycle and so the loop goes on (Figure 5.1).

This is often why when we try to change our own or someone else's behaviour, it doesn't work, because we're only dealing with a small percentage of the cycle – the behaviour – rather than addressing what's driving that behaviour underneath the surface. We are in fact addressing the symptoms again and not the causes.

The same editing system also directs how we feel about the information we're receiving. For example, we're more likely to take on board information that affirms or supports our existing beliefs, than we are to take on board something that doesn't agree with our way of thinking. We appear to be programmed this way to avoid our brains seething with information overload. However, the only problem with this beautiful system is that we rarely question the process going on behind the scenes and can end up spending most of our lives walking around with a semi-comatose view of the world.

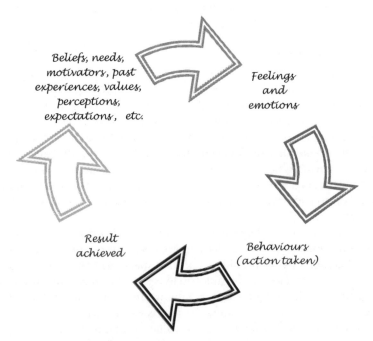

Figure 5.1 The behavioural cycle

Our own behaviour

So what does this have to do with stress and energy levels? Quite simply, you are in control of your own editing system. If you choose to filter an experience through a negative and stressful editing system, you will experience a stressful outcome. However, if you choose to filter an experience through a different editing system, you'll get a whole other experience.

This doesn't mean that you can't experience a stressful event. We all do at various times, and some of these events can even be quite stimulating. But the secret as to whether or not a negative experience remains on your stress radar for you is based on choice. You can choose how you view a situation, event or person. If you want to view and hold on to it as a stressful experience, you will do; and your brain will continue to reinforce this belief for you.

So what are energy-depleting behaviours?

Energy-depleting behaviours actually require more energy to maintain than do positive behaviours. They also create a stress response in our bodies, and when conducted on a consistent basis, can begin to affect us at a physiological and psychological level.

To test this, think of a time when you've been angry with someone or worried about something for any considerable length of time. Did you find the experience exhausting? Did you feel depleted physically, emotionally and psychologically after a while?

Examples of energy-depleting behaviour

- Power plays/game playing
- Lying
- Abusive or addictive behaviour
- Controlling or manipulating
- Gossiping
- Non-assertive or aggressive behaviours
- Blaming
- Worrying
- Arguing
- Judging others.

When we recognize these energy-depleting behaviours in ourselves, we have a choice. We can either choose to stay in this unhappy space, or we can choose to let it go and move on. However, the more we've become addicted to these heightened emotional states (and the consequent adrenaline that's now pumping around our system), the harder we'll find it to change. But when we're expending energy on negative behaviour patterns, we're wasting energy; it's that simple.

If, on the other hand, our behaviour is having a positive influence on our life, or on another person's life, then that is energy wisely invested.

Examples of energy-enhancing behaviour

- Helping others
- Making time for yourself
- Giving for no reward or gain
- Caring for others
- Empowering self and others
- Learning from experiences
- Assertive behaviours
- Accepting responsibility
- Not judging others
- Resolving conflict
- Taking ownership.

Other people's behaviour

It's been documented that some 90 per cent of the conflict or stress we experience is often due to our perception of another person's behaviour as being either 'right' or 'wrong', and we may use this yardstick to measure or judge others' behaviour. I am the first to say that it's no easy task to learn how to detach ourselves emotionally from other people's behaviour. It took me a long time to learn how to do it and there are still times when I can feel my nostrils flaring as a result of something someone else has said or done. But in terms of preserving our precious energy reserves, not to mention our sanity, it's a critical skill to learn and something I'll try to help you with in Chapter 8.

But before we leave this topic, here's something else to consider. People can only treat you in the way you allow them to treat you. No one can do something 'to you' without your permission. In every inter-action we have, we're establishing a set of rules or boundaries that say, 'This is how I want to be treated or will allow you to treat me'. So, if you feel someone's behaviour towards you is unfair, consider how much you've allowed them to rewrite those boundaries for you. As children, we learnt how to push boundaries to see what we could get away with, and as adults we may continue to apply this technique.

Now, let's take a pulse check on these areas of your external world. Bear in mind that the more honest you are in your answers, the more you'll get out of these two pulse checks.

Behaviour: Energy Pulse Check

Our own behaviour
How many of the energy-depleting behaviours could you identify with/ recognize in yourself?

Has it always been this way for you? If not, what has changed?

Where do you think these negative patterns of behaviour originated? (e.g. past experiences, beliefs, conditioning, rules you have written for yourself or others, etc.)

Are these still applicable to you now?

What pay-off(s) are you gaining from continuing this/these pattern(s) of behaviour?

How could you gain the same pay-off(s) from a more positive pattern(s) of behaviour?

What is your motivation for wanting to change this/these negative pattern(s) of behaviour?

What steps can you put in place to start breaking this/these cycle(s)?

How many of the energy-enhancing behaviours do you consistently demonstrate?

How do you feel when you engage in these behaviours?

What steps could you put in place to increase these energy-enhancing behaviours?

Other people's behaviour
How much of your own energy do you spend on reacting to other people's behaviour?

Has it always been this way for you? And if not, what has changed?

When someone behaves in a way that upsets you, how do you usually react?

What are the 'films' that are playing in your mind at the time?

How do you feel afterwards?

What 'yardstick' are you measuring other people's behaviours by?

How would you feel if someone was measuring your behaviour by the same yardstick?

How else could you view other people's behaviour?

What's one thing you could do today to start changing how you react to other people's behaviours (i.e. to start responding as opposed to reacting)?

My behaviour ROEI assessment

1 = little or no ROEI
2 = moderate ROEI
3 = above average or maximum ROEI

Energy Investment Area	ROEI Rating
My own behaviour	
Other people's behaviour	

Social conforms

We touched on this area when we talked about our clan/tribe, and the pressure we may feel from its members to conform. But this time we're going to briefly explore the topic from a wider perspective.

All societies have certain rules that offer us guidelines about what is generally considered acceptable or unacceptable behaviour, and we can choose to conform to these guidelines or not. These days, these guidelines have become much less restrictive than they would have been, say, 100 years ago, but there are still certain unspoken expectations that appear to exist in society that evolve around how men and women are supposed to behave.

I'm not talking here about the law and what is defined as being legal or illegal, but about the subtle, often unspoken, rules that are often handed down from one generation to another. For example, expectations around how men and women are supposed to engage in the dating game; what is acceptable for a man as opposed to a woman when it comes to sexual behaviour; expectations around when we should get married, settle down or have children; perceptions about who should be the primary breadwinner in a relationship or primary caretaker of children; views about people who may choose to remain single, live in different types of relationships, or opt not to have children, and so on.

These external pressures to conform can often create internal conflict as we expend huge amounts of energy trying to conform.

To know if you're operating under a system of inappropriate or questionable rules, keep an eye out for words like 'should', 'shouldn't', 'can't', 'must', 'need to' or 'have to'. Whether you're saying them, or someone else is saying them, any sentence with these words in it can indicate a rule by which you're living your life.

For example, 'I should have children by the time I'm 30'. With this 'rule', somewhere along the line a belief was either inherited or born that said this is the way it 'should' be. Because we're not used to questioning these unwritten rules, if we had this rule, we have probably never actually asked ourselves whether it's valid or where it came from, let alone if it's still applicable.

By replacing these 'rule words' with new ones like 'choosing' – for example, 'I choose to go to the gym' rather than 'I should go to the gym' – you put a whole new spin on a topic. It is a spin that will make you feel more empowered when it comes to the decisions you're making in life; and with empowerment comes less stress and more energy.

Social conforms: Energy Pulse Check

Consider your own life. Do you feel you are, or have been, living your life in accordance with rules that you may have inherited or have become conditioned to?

Has it always been this way for you and, if not, what has changed?

How many of these rules did you create for yourself and why?

Are these rules still acceptable to you today?

Do you expend energy trying either to push against these rules or conform to them?

How does this make you feel?

Do you know why these rules are not acceptable or suitable for you and the life you want to live?

What new, more positive 'rules' could you replace them with?

My social conforms ROEI assessment

1 = little or no ROEI
2 = moderate ROEI
3 = above average or maximum ROEI

Energy Investment Area	ROEI Rating
Social conforms	

Family

Like our relationships with other people, our family members can deplete our energy and be a cause of stress in our lives, as we simply try to get along, argue, fight, battle, play games or just plain avoid them. Or these relationships can be a great source of comfort to us and give us energy. With members of our family, we're probably less likely to want to give up on these relationships altogether and to walk away from them in the way we might do with a friend who has become an energy vampire.

There are so many variables as to why we find it difficult to get along with family members, and while we may be able to repair some of these relationships by discussing our concerns or varying viewpoints or just agreeing to disagree, some issues between relatives may feel beyond repair.

Like our section on intimate relationships and finding love, this is a topic that goes well beyond the confines of this book. There are many books and sources to consult depending on your specific family issues or concerns. So, if this is an area of great stress for you, do seek out any guidance you need, either to help you work through your own issues, or to begin to repair your relationships within your family unit.

Family: Energy Pulse Check

How would you describe your relationships with your immediate family?

Which member(s) do you feel you have the best relationship with and why?

Has it always been this way?

If not, what has changed?

Which member(s) of your family do you feel your relationship could be better with and why?

Has it always been this way?

If not, what has changed?

If you leave this/these relationship(s) in its/their current state(s), how would you feel?

If you leave this/these relationship(s) in its/their current state(s), how would you feel five and ten years from now?

Would you regret never finding a solution to this/these problem(s)?

What is one thing you could do today that would make the biggest difference to how you feel about this/these family member(s)?

What is one thing you could do today that would make the biggest difference to how you respond to this/these family member(s)?

If this was not a member of your own family, how would you advise someone else to approach the problem(s)?

My family ROEI assessment

As you may have many relatives to consider within your family unit, I've left the assessment box blank for you to complete and to apply the relevant ROEI rating to each family member as you wish.

1 = little or no ROEI
2 = moderate ROEI
3 = above average or maximum ROEI

Energy Investment Area	ROEI Rating

Community

Welcome to the final area of your external world: community. People become involved in their communities for a variety of reasons – for example, wanting to have a sense of belonging to their local area, having a desire to give something back to their area, or having a wish to support a local volunteer initiative or charity.

Regardless of our motivation for becoming involved, most of the benefits gained from a stress/energy balance perspective are positive ones that energize us and give us an intrinsic 'feel-good' factor.

For some people, however, what begins as an energizing experience can turn progressively into an energy-depleting one, as people find themselves over-committed to numerous community initiatives or activities. For these people, good intentions have led to a new cause of stress in their lives, as they try to juggle these additional activities with their existing work and family commitments.

Again, it's a question of balance. If you're involved and enjoying the experience – great. If you're not involved and would like to be – find ways of getting involved. If you're not involved and have no desire to be – then that's fine too. And if you're involved and feel over-committed, find ways of cutting back on either your areas of focus or the amount of time you've allocated to this work. This way you'll start to enjoy the experience again and you'll be able to give more quality time to your initiatives than you're probably able to at the moment.

Community: Energy Pulse Check

Are you involved in volunteer or community initiatives in your local area?

Do you find your involvement energizing or stressful?

What benefits or needs does your involvement give you/meet for you?

If you have always wanted to become involved but haven't, what has prevented you from doing so?

What would need to change to enable you to do these activities?

Are there other ways you can become involved that you may not have considered?

If you're feeling over-committed at the moment, how can you streamline your level of involvement?

What other activities could give you the same benefits or enjoyment but offer you greater flexibility in terms of your commitment?

My community ROEI assessment

Energy Investment Area	ROEI Rating
Community	

Finally...

If you have an area of your life in your external world that has not been covered, I'm sorry to have missed it. But use your understanding of how the question and assessment process works to make your own ROEI assessment on this area and add it in.

Now let's turn to the fascinating world of our internal energy reserve!

6

Internal energy reserve: an endless supply?

Topic Teasers

- Do you understand how your internal energy centres are continually affecting and influencing one another?
- Could you identify the various aspects of each centre?
- Do you know why your spirituality is critical to maintaining energy balance?
- Do you know how your psychological energy may be impacting on how you feel and the results you're achieving in life?
- Do you know what the effect of continually operating at maximum capacity might be on you?

A quick word on action planning

With the help of the last two chapters, you've identified and explored aspects of your external world that may be creating stress for you, and affecting your energy levels and general well-being. But this is only half of the stress/energy equation. The other half involves understanding more about the effects that these areas of stress may be having on you and your energy reserve, which we'll do in this chapter.

There are three options, depending on how you want to approach your Action Plan:

What, not how

You may be feeling that you'd rather focus your time and energy on the stress factors in your external world at this stage, and come back later to addressing the internal aspects of how you're feeling. If so, feel free to flick on to the next chapter on action planning.

How, not what

Here, you may feel that the factors in your external world are not causing you too much stress at this time, and you'd rather focus your energy and time on changing how you feel internally. If this is the case, then for you it's less about what's in your life, and more about how you're living that life. If so, do stay with this chapter before moving on to the next chapter to create your Action Plan.

A pick-and-mix approach

You may prefer to tackle both areas at the same time, which is a commendable goal to have. However, depending on the level of change you want to initiate in your external world, you may want to take a pick-and-mix approach to your Action Plan. For example, you could work on one smaller aspect of your external world, while tackling one aspect of your well-being. This step-by-step approach will help you to use the momentum you're gaining with each change to make bigger changes later on. If this is your preferred choice, continue with this chapter, and we'll explore your Action Plan in more detail in the next chapter.

ROEI ratings

For this part of the book, you won't be asked to rate each of your three energy centres using the ROEI ratings scale, but you will be asked to consider a series of questions for each one in the form of Energy Pulse Checks. As previously in this book, these questions have been designed to help you to identify and further understand each of your energy centres and the amount of attention you may be paying to each one.

An endless supply?

Earlier in the book I introduced you to the three internal energy centres – physical, psychological and spiritual – that make up your energy reserve, and their combined role in providing you with the energy you need each and every day.

Not only do they fulfil this role, but they also help you to define who you are and your view of the world around you. Yet, for the most part, we don't give them any conscious thought at all, and give even less thought to ways of replenishing this vital energy supply. In short, we take them for granted. Much in the same way that we turn on a tap and expect to see water, so we just expect our energy supply always to be there for us. It's only when things go wrong, and we start to feel the effects of energy imbalance, that we start to pay this vital source any attention (a bit like shutting the gate after our resuscitated horse has bolted for the hills).

Interconnecting centres

To function on a day-to-day basis, you require energy – physical energy to move around and to meet the physical demands of your external world; psychological energy to think, experience emotions and process information; and spiritual energy to provide you with a sense of identity and inner well-being (Figure 6.1).

For example, we all know how it feels when we're feeling physically energized and alive. We have heaps of stamina and this increase in physical energy influences how we feel at a psychological and emotional level too. The same can be said when we're feeling physically tired. This can affect our psychological and emotional states and we often feel low, fed up, down in the dumps, distracted and lethargic.

We draw on each of our three energy centres every day, all day, as they impact on and influence one another.

Think of them as a three-legged milking stool. If one of the legs were missing, we'd be unable to stay balanced. The same can be said of our energy reserve; when we place all of our focus on only one aspect of it, we decrease the importance of balance in the energy equation.

So, to feel truly energized, we need to be accessing and re-energizing each of our three energy centres.

It's almost impossible to separate this intricate relationship of interdependence, and neither should we want to, because, when combined,

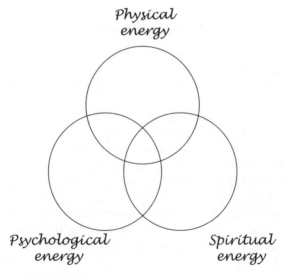

Figure 6.1 Your internal energy reserve

these three centres create the magical and complex essence of who we are. That essence is unique to each one of us. It's our energy fingerprint, or DNA, if you like, and defines who we are, how we feel, how we behave and the results we achieve in life.

My goal for you in this chapter is to help you to move towards a more proactive approach to your energy game.

Pulse checking your internal energy reserve

It might help to think of your mobile phone, strange as it may sound. On our mobile phone, we have a small indicator that tells us when the battery is running low. Just imagine how easy it would be if you had one of these implanted in your wrist for each of your energy centres. You'd know straight away if you were running a little low on fuel and be able to recharge that exact same energy centre whenever you needed to. But as I'm talking in the realms of science fiction here, you'll just have to use your imagination instead, and the Energy Pulse Checks provided, to start building a picture of what it is like to feel fully energized and what it might feel like when you're falling out of balance.

Let's begin with our spiritual energy centre.

Spiritual energy centre

Providing critical balance

Spiritual energy means different things to different people. For some it can be defined within the context of religious beliefs. For others, it is something that they sense within themselves, a sense of identity or internal well-being.

For the purposes of this book, I'm defining spiritual energy as 'our innate desire to feel a sense of connection to something greater than ourselves; a feeling of belonging, peace of mind, or awareness of a higher level of existence that goes beyond our normal physical or psychological being'.

Spiritual energy

- A sense of identity
- Religious beliefs
- Spirituality
- A sense of well-being
- A feeling of 'connection'.

Sometimes described as the soul, we're often unaware of this deep inner need to feel a sense of connection to something that we can't quite put our finger on. All we know is that when we have it, we appear to have a greater understanding of who we are, why we're here, and our place in the world.

We can also easily describe the sense of inner peace and calm that we feel when we do finally manage to put our finger on it, and what it feels like when it's missing – using expressions like 'there's got to be something more than this', as we attempt to describe a gnawing feeling that seems to originate from somewhere deep inside us.

This is what can happen when our spiritual energy is being under-used. It has a critical role to play in the stress/energy equation, and when we ignore it, we can experience a sense of 'something' being out of place even if we're often unable to articulate exactly what it is that feels out of place.

Our spirituality is what completes us as a person, and when we engage this critical energy centre, we feel relaxed but at the same time energized and alive, and we can feel a greater sense of purpose about our lives than we may have ever felt before. We stop sweating about the small stuff and find peace of mind in this quiet inner silence. It's the energy centre that brings calm to chaos, slows down our thinking, and helps us to connect to our intuition, which plays a key role in helping us to achieve the critical balance of cognitive and intuitive thinking; a valuable tool in the decision-making process.

Defining what spirituality means to each of us is our own very private journey. There are no hard-and-fast rules around what it needs to look like, what beliefs we need to hold, or how long your personal journey should take. It doesn't even matter if your interpretation of what spirituality means for you makes no sense to other people, as long as it makes sense to you. That's what's really important.

Signs of imbalance

Perhaps this is best summed up by my own experience: 'I felt empty inside; hollow, like an empty shell. It was as if I had lost my soul and the very essence of who I was as a person. I felt alone, disconnected from everything around me and lost.'

Therefore based on my own experiences, and other people's, common signs of an imbalance in our spiritual energy centre can include:

- a lack of inner peace and calm
- loss of a sense of meaning
- a sense of futility

- loss of idealism
- feeling you've lost your 'soul', 'anchor' or 'compass'
- feeling you've lost your path, or your way
- a sense that something bigger than yourself is missing.

Now let's explore this aspect of your internal energy reserve with an Energy Pulse Check.

Spiritual energy centre: Energy Pulse Check

What does spirituality mean to you?

What does spirituality bring to your life?

In what ways do you/are you engaging with your spiritual energy centre each day?

How many of the signs of imbalance could you identify with?

What methods do you use to 'top up' this part of your energy reserve?

Do you feel more balanced when you have been, or are being, re-energized in this critical part of your energy reserve?

If you've never engaged this part of your energy reserve, what methods are you using to develop your inner sense of identity, or to gain feelings of calm, peace and well-being?

If you've never engaged this part of your energy reserve, do you feel as if something is missing in your life?

If yes, how would you describe this feeling?

What steps could you take to address this imbalance?

Psychological energy centre

Now it's time to explore the next component of your energy reserve: your psychological energy centre. Table 6.1 gives a breakdown of what psychological energy is.

Table 6.1 Psychological energy

Conscious or cognitive thought:	Mental agility
	Acquisition of knowledge
	Processing of information
Subconscious thought:	A 'filtering system'
	Our 'internal dialogue'
	Ego
	Self-actualization
	Self-efficacy
	Self-perception
	Conscience
	Personality
	Perception
	Beliefs, motivators, values, etc.
	Rules
	Expectations
	Stress reaction and coping
	mechanisms
Emotional energy:	Emotional processing, resilience,
	expression and management

Conscious or cognitive thought

This area of our psychological energy represents the conscious use and application of thought in our daily lives as we access, acquire and process knowledge and information.

Examples of this in action include consciously deciding to think about something or someone; accessing existing information and applying it to a given situation; making decisions; deciding to learn something new or trying to understand a new concept or idea.

As you'll know from your own life, we expend a massive amount of energy in this area every day, as we make decisions and access and process information without apparently giving it a second thought. It operates at lightning speed as it works with us during the day, processing not only all of the new information coming at us, but all of the other 'stuff' too, such as when we need to pick the kids up from school; what we're going to have for dinner; what we're going to do at the weekend; what happened during the day; what went well and what we wish we'd handled better.

Adam

I experienced short-term memory loss, low self-confidence, and lost the ability to think clearly as well as to be a visionary leader. I was unable to support other people as I was busy trying to support myself. I also indulged in escapism and became an angry, cynical and bitter man.

We process literally thousands of pieces of information every day. That's one busy internal dialogue going on up there. So it's no wonder that this energy centre can feel exhausted occasionally as it struggles to keep up with the demands we place on it.

Our minds, like our bodies, need to rest. By freeing up space in our minds, we're more able to release creative energy, to stay mentally alert for longer, and to create a greater balance of cognitive and intuitive thinking.

As discussed in the last chapter, we have an in-built editing system that provides structure and form to our thoughts, using our beliefs, past experiences, motivators and values. So every piece of information you're consciously thinking about goes through this editing and filtering process. This links with another aspect of our psychological energy centre: subconscious thought.

Subconscious thought

Only around 10 per cent of what's going on inside your head ever manifests into visible behaviours, words or actions that are observable to other people. This also means that you can only see 10 per cent of what's really going on inside someone else's head.

Not a lot really, is it? Like an iceberg, the rest of the party is all going on below the surface, in the form of thoughts (conscious thought) and subconscious filtering. There are many layers to this internal filtering process and we access most of them all the time without even being aware of it.

Our editing system provides us with many services; for example it:

- selects and provides us with information that helps us to make sense of the world around us;
- guides our emotions and feelings about things, situations and people;
- directs our subsequent actions, when we do them and how;
- creates 'rules' for us to live by based on our conditioning and past experiences;

- responds to the needs of our ego;
- contains a conceptualized image or blueprint of our idealized selves and the people we aspire to be in life;
- houses our perceptions about ourselves and guides our decisions in line with what we've told ourselves is possible or impossible;
- establishes expectations about ourselves and others and uses this yardstick to judge our own and other people's behaviour;
- defines our personality and the outward display we show to the world;
- provides a home for the things we value and desire;
- defines and creates our perceptions of reality.

That's a pretty impressive list, and that's only a few of the many services our filtering system provides for us. This list could go on and on, because our subconscious is a bit like the universe; it's limitless and still has many uncharted territories yet to be explored. However, even looking at the above list, it's easy to see why this filtering system plays such a critical role for us when it comes to conscious thought.

Together, these two aspects are on stand-by and full alert 24 hours a day; even when we're sleeping they're still active, as they diligently process information from the day and create new 'files' for our brains' filing cabinets.

So it's not surprising that we can often find ourselves using expressions like feeling 'brain dead' or suffering from 'brain overload' or 'brain drain' to describe how we feel when we've been over-using these two hardworking aspects of our psychological energy centre.

When we feel mentally exhausted, and all we want to do is to get out of our own heads, stop thinking and shut down all the chatter for a while, these are all indicators that it's time to recharge.

Margaret
I suffered from depression; worrying about anything and everything and feeling angry. I also experienced a fear of never being a success again and all with a terrible overriding fear of failure.

Emotional energy

Emotions may span both conscious and subconscious thought. At a conscious level, we can choose to feel a certain way about something or someone. However, as we've seen, the emotions we decide to feel or display are often dictated by our internal editing system. Hence, our emotions span both the conscious and subconscious components of our psychological energy centre.

Our emotions play a huge role in how we feel about ourselves and our lives in general, and can therefore influence whether we're feeling energized or depleted in terms of our energy levels.

Let's use the example of being in love. We all know how we feel when we're in this ecstatic headspace: happy, content, alive, energized and at peace. We stop worrying about little things and may feel in love with the whole world. This is an example of how an emotional state can energize us.

Now think about a time when you've experienced the opposite; perhaps at the end of a relationship. Apart from the negative emotions you might feel towards your ex, you might also feel deflated, down, depressed, tearful and emotionally drained. When we're experiencing these types of emotions, we're still expending a huge amount of energy, but not in a positive way.

This simple example shows how our emotional states can influence our energy levels, and I'm sure we can think of many other examples, but the truth is, when we're feeling good about ourselves and our lives, we feel lighter and more energized than we do when we're experiencing frustration and stress. These negative emotions can actually make us feel physically and psychologically heavy and weighted down.

Mary
Not only did I feel physically tired, but I had lost all of my enthusiasm. I didn't want to go to work in the morning and I felt very emotional. My emotions were accentuated and I felt like I was on an emotional rollercoaster.

Emotional energy: a second level

As well as experiencing our primary emotions, we also experience another level of emotion – secondary emotions. Let me explain.

Suppose you're feeling angry about someone or something, but you have created a rule in your editing system that tells you that you 'shouldn't' be feeling angry in this way. This 'rule' then triggers a second layer of emotional energy – that is, feeling sad or angry about the fact that you're feeling angry.

In this example, your secondary emotion is sadness or anger. So, emotions can often have two layers to them, depending on what's happening at the time and the editing process they've passed through. In this scenario, we're expending twice the amount of energy not only on the primary emotion (feeling angry), but on the secondary layer too (feeling sad or angry about feeling angry).

Emotional energy: more dimensions

Here are two more aspects of our emotional energy that can affect our stress/energy levels – how we process emotions, and our ability to manage our emotional states.

One effective way of doing this is to become an observer of your own emotional states – detaching from the emotional state you're experiencing and analysing what's going on and why. When we do this, we give ourselves the opportunity to learn from our experiences, move on from them and then let them go. I'm not talking about becoming a soulless android here and removing your emotion chip. It's more about allowing yourself to experience an emotion, but then learning how to let it go, and not choosing to hold on to the negative emotional states that can deplete your energy levels and increase your stress levels.

James
I was very emotional, anxious and started to suffer from self-doubt, para-noia and a loss of self-confidence. I wanted to leave my work role, but no longer trusted my ability to judge a situation. It was like a detached, dream-like state which fused with reality.

Emotional resilience refers to the extent to which we're able to 'bounce back' from emotional setbacks. Our ability to take on the role of observer and to learn from our various emotional states lies at the centre of how quickly we may, or may not, bounce back from an emotional upset. The more we allow ourselves to wallow, be swept away or become overwhelmed by our emotions, the harder we may find it to regain our balance.

Another handy tool in the emotional armoury is the acceptance that we experience a myriad of emotions, not just a few. If asked to list common emotions we would probably identify love, anger, sadness or sorrow, happiness, surprise, fear, disgust and guilt. However, every emotion exists on a continuum where its opposite emotional state exists at the other end. For example, we wouldn't be able to fully understand happiness if we had never experienced feeling unhappy, or understand feelings of calm if we had never felt unsettled.

By accepting that we can experience a vast range of emotions, and that there are no right or wrong emotions, we can allow ourselves to experience them without trying to fence them in with rules about what we 'should' or 'shouldn't' be feeling. This way we're able to use our emotional states as yet another way of learning more about ourselves and why we feel the emotions we feel.

A final word on emotions

When it comes to the stress/energy equation, we can see how closely these three components of our psychological energy centre are linked, as each one feeds into, inspires or affects the others, all day, every day.

Together they can either work for us, or against us. But the good news is that you have complete control over which way the wind could blow. The choice is always in your own hands.

Remember, the stress response is only the response you choose to have to an external pressure. It's not written in stone that it has to be a certain way. If you choose to engage in constant negative internal chatter in your mind about yourself, other people or situations, then you choose to create and maintain negative thoughts that will affect how you feel at an emotional level too. Collectively, all this dense energy will only serve to deplete your overall psychological energy, and eventually your physical energy too – not to mention increasing the stress you're already experiencing.

So, as we can see, the links between these three components of our psychological energy centres are vast and never-ending. Our minds are in a continuous state of movement, as we access, process and apply every thought we have, whether it originates in our conscious or our subconscious.

Over the years there has been, and will probably continue to be, much debate about which of these aspects drives the other; whether we'll ever find the answers we seek, I have no idea. For me, the mystery of how and why we work the way we do only adds to the fascination of this topic.

Before you complete your next Energy Pulse Check, let's take a moment to consider what it might look like if this energy centre was feeling in need of a recharge.

Psychological energy centre: signs of imbalance

General signals that our psychological energy centre is under stress can include:

- feelings of 'brain drain', feeling 'brain dead' or general mental exhaustion
- lack of concentration or feeling easily distracted
- an inability to cope with everyday stressors
- withdrawal or detachment from people
- insecurity about competency levels
- an increasing lack of self-confidence or self-esteem
- a decreasing belief in self and own abilities

- depression
- short-term memory loss
- feelings of guilt
- over-confidence or risk taking
- hypochondria
- feelings of grief or an overwhelming sense of loss
- low morale (and low productivity as a result).

Emotional signals of imbalance

Signals with regard to emotional imbalance may be a result of our physical or psychological symptoms, and can include feelings of:

- emotional exhaustion or loss of emotional control
- cynicism, negativism or pessimism
- resentment, stagnation or boredom
- sadness, disillusionment or feelings of failure
- anger or frustration
- indifference or emotional detachment
- powerlessness or hopelessness
- irritability or impatience
- anxiety or restlessness
- dissatisfaction or disappointment
- being overworked and/or under-valued
- suspicion or paranoia
- being 'overwhelmed'
- increased uncertainty about self and own abilities.

Behavioural signals of imbalance

Behavioural signals also appear to have a strong relationship with our psychological signals, as well as our emotional signals, as the intensity of our emotional states will often drive the level to which a behavioural signal is shown. They can include:

- increased taking of stimulants, e.g. coffee, cigarettes, alcohol, etc.
- increased escapist behaviours, e.g. drinking, drug taking, excess partying, compulsive shopping, etc.
- indecisiveness or procrastination
- reduced productivity and increased absenteeism
- working harder, faster and for longer periods
- hyperactivity or erratic/unpredictable responses or behaviours
- existing personality problems that become accentuated
- increased harshness towards others
- resistance to change or a lack of flexibility

- loss of empathy or concern for others
- decreased communication
- increased marital or family conflict
- accident proneness or increased error rate
- weakened moral or emotional constraints
- becoming obsessive about work.

It's my feeling that links exist between many of our psychological symptoms. For example, our lack of concentration can lead to an increased error rate, which in turn can affect our self-esteem and self-confidence. Or, emotional changes can ultimately create feelings of self-doubt about ourselves, our abilities and our overall competency levels, as well as feelings of guilt and low morale. As these symptoms increase, we may feel an increasing need to withdraw from public view and may start to isolate ourselves from friends and family.

From my research and interviews, I also think that the degree of severity with which you experience any of these signals may also depend on how long you've been experiencing prolonged or excessive stress, and how long your energy reserve has been in a state of imbalance.

It's now time to do three Energy Pulse Checks, one for each aspect of your psychological energy centre.

Psychological energy centre: Energy Pulse Check

Conscious thought

How often do you take a break during the day to allow your brain to have some down time?

How many of the general psychological signals of imbalance could you identify with?

How many of the behavioural signals of imbalance could you identify with?

What effects do you notice when you try to push beyond your natural reserves (i.e. trying to complete work or activities that require mental agility when your mind feels tired)?

Describe how you feel when you're feeling psychologically (or mentally) engaged and alert.

When did you last feel like this?

Subconscious thought

What negative and positive internal dialogue do you have?

In what way(s) do you feel this internal dialogue might be affecting your overall psychological energy centre (including emotional energy)?

What methods do you/could you use to break this/these negative internal dialogue(s) when you experience them?

What 'rules' have you created that are working for you, and which rules may be working against you?

Are these rules still applicable to you and the life you want to live?

If not, what new rules could you replace them with?

What role do you feel your editing system may be playing in terms of how you see yourself and the world around you?

Is this view of the world working for or against you?

What methods do you use to re-energize this aspect of your psychological energy centre (subconscious thought)?

Emotional energy

How many of the emotional signals of imbalance could you identify with?

Has it always been this way for you? And if not, what's changed?

In what way do you feel your negative and positive emotions are influencing how you feel on a day-to-day basis?

How aware are you of your various emotional states and their origins? (Have you already been playing the role of the observer?)

What 'rules' (if any) have you written for yourself when it comes to experiencing emotions?

What emotions do you feel it is not OK to experience and why?

What could you do to learn how to handle negative emotions more productively?

What can you learn from the various emotions you experience?

How easy do you find it to bounce back from an emotional upset?

What methods could you put in place to build your emotional resilience?

What depletes or energizes you emotionally?

General

How can you use this information about yourself?

What methods can you put in place to become the observer of your psychological energy centre?

In what ways can monitoring this aspect of your internal energy help you?

What physical and spiritual benefits might you receive in return?

Physical energy: high, low or neutral?

When we talk about our energy, we often use expressions like 'feeling hyped up', 'feeling wired', 'running on empty' or 'our battery feeling flat'. It would appear that when we experience either a high or a low in our energy, we tend to notice it more than we do if we're somewhere in the middle, or when we're running in neutral.

Physical energy

- General health and well-being
- Strength
- Stamina
- Resilience
- Fitness.

When our energy is high, even if much of it is often chemically induced, we can have a tendency to take our energy for granted. We just keep tapping into it and expending energy like there's no tomorrow, and no consequence. After all, it'll always be there, won't it?

I have a theory about this which I'd like to share. I think we don't notice our 'neutral' mode as much because we're not yet feeling the effects on our other energy centres as much as we would if we were feeling 'wired' or 'flat'. Think about it for a moment. As discussed earlier, if you're feeling great in one of your energy centres, then chances are you're feeling pretty buzzy across the other two as well, and the same goes for the opposite ripple effect. But if we're operating in a high zone and we're feeling good about it, how might this be a problem in the long term?

Operating at maximum capacity

There seems to be an increasing emphasis these days on 'high performance' or 'operating at maximum performance'. Whether these expressions originated in the boardroom and spilled over into our private lives or the other way around, I'm not sure; but whichever way it occurred, we're certainly trying to fit more into our days than we did, say, ten or twenty years ago. We're engaged in an endless juggling act of multiple commitments and priorities, which is where the art of chemical abuse comes in as we try to squeeze more mileage out of our physical energy than we were ever designed to have in the first place.

Most stress-related research tells us that when we're operating at 'optimal capacity', we're balancing somewhere between too much, and too little stress arousal, and when we're in this mode we're generally performing at our best. We're feeling engaged, alive and switched on at every level.

Now this might sound like a great place to be, but there is a downside to this equation and it's this: when we're in this mode all the time, we have little or no spare capacity from an energy perspective. It's a bit like driving with your foot on the accelerator all the time. When you need a little extra 'oomph' to get you up a hill, it's just not there because you're already driving at your car's full capacity.

When this happens, you're starting to push your physical energy limits beyond their natural capabilities. You'll only be able to do this for so long before you'll start to feel the negative side effects of excessive energy depletion, such as tension headaches, backache and insomnia. And as we've identified, quicker than you can say pass the Valium, these physical side effects can start to affect the rest of our energy reserve at a psychological and spiritual level too.

Bethany

Physical symptoms I experienced included insomnia (I was getting between one and two hours' sleep a night); chest pains on a daily basis; migraines; a continuous tension in my stomach; poor digestion; hair loss; numbness and pins and needles down the left-hand side of my body.

Sooner or later, we start running on empty, but ironically, by then, we've often become so used to feeling this way that we just think this is our new 'normal' and take no action to remedy the situation, and continue to ignore the constant warning signals. It's often only when we finally take a break that we realize just how physically (and psychologically) exhausted we've become. So what could some of these physical warning signs look like?

Physical energy: signals of imbalance

Signals of physical energy imbalance are as wide as they are varied, but here are some common ones:

- fatigue, exhaustion or feeling drained
- digestive problems or ulcers
- headaches or migraines
- high blood pressure
- frequent or lingering illness
- muscle tension or aching muscles
- back pain
- nausea
- heart problems
- increased or shallow breathing
- high cholesterol levels
- insomnia or sleeping more than usual
- weight gain or loss
- sexual dysfunction
- asthma or allergies
- skin conditions (e.g. acne, eczema)
- menstrual problems.

The more we allow these symptoms to continue without addressing the balance, the more they'll begin to affect other areas of our energy reserve at a psychological and spiritual level, and so the downward cycle continues.

Physical energy centre: Energy Pulse Check

How often do you feel you're operating at maximum capacity?

How many of the physical warning signals can you identify with?

When was the last time you felt physically energized and what did it feel like?

How often do you recharge this energy centre and what methods do you use?

How much spare capacity do you feel you have right now to tap into?

What does this tell you about how you're currently using this energy centre?

How often do you feel physically exhausted?

How long have you felt this way?

If it hasn't always been this way for you, what has changed?

This brings us to the end of our chapter on your internal energy reserve. There's been a lot of information to take on board, and hopefully a lot to think about too. But in this case, psychological stimulation is a good thing if it's going to help you to learn how to manage your stress and energy more effectively in the future.

So, without further ado, let's move you on to your action planning, where you'll have a choice of three approaches, depending on how you want to focus your time and energy.

In Chapter 8 I've included some ideas and techniques for some of the areas we've discussed in the book. Where an area falls outside my area of expertise, I've made a few suggestions on possible approaches you could take.

7

Creating your Action Plan

Topic Teasers

- Do you want to learn a simple five-step process to help you to maintain a balanced state of energy and to build an energy reserve at the same time?
- Do you want to learn how to extend beyond your normal energy boundaries and be able to recover quickly and easily?
- Do you want to achieve peace of mind so that you can cope with whatever life throws at you?

At the end of this chapter, you'll find a template for you to complete your Action Plan; and, as discussed earlier, there are three possible ways you can use it.

What, not how

You want to address factors of your external world that are creating stress for you at this time before looking at your internal energy balance. If this is your approach of choice, then focus your attention at this time on Part A of this chapter, which contains some tips on how to get things moving and a recommended approach.

How, not what

You want to address how you're feeling internally and how you're experiencing your external world at this time. If this is your approach of choice, then focus your attention on Part B of this chapter, which also provides hints on how to get things moving and a recommended plan of attack.

A pick-and-mix approach

You would like to tackle aspects of both your external and internal world at the same time. There's no right or wrong way of approaching your Action Plan, but please do be conscious of taking on too much at the same time, especially if you have quite a few factors in your external world to work through. I want to see you succeed, not increase your current stress levels; so if you decide to take this approach, I recommend taking one bite-sized chunk at a time, and working out what will make the biggest difference to you at this particular time. Then use this success to make the next change and so on.

Regardless of which approach you decide to take, it's important to keep your Action Plan visible at all times. This ensures your plan:

- is a living document that can be added to or amended as needed;
- is not hidden from view or forgotten about;
- becomes part of your daily routine, just like checking your diary each day to see what activities or tasks you need to do;
- is monitored on a regular basis;
- is given the level of importance in your life that you deserve.

Donna
For me, I decided to address the internal imbalance that I felt physically, psychologically and spiritually, before tackling the external world and my primary stress areas.

This was only because I knew that I wasn't in the best headspace to make considered decisions about my external world at that time. I was worried that I might make reactive and emotional decisions that I'd later regret.

Step by step

From my own experience, and that of my clients, when making changes in our lives we can sometimes feel a little overwhelmed, especially if we have more than one area that we want to make changes in.

Alternatively, if we're feeling a little frustrated and impatient about wanting to see change happen quickly, we can end up taking a scattergun approach as we make random changes left, right and centre in the hope that we'll finish them all off quicker.

Although this latter approach may work for some people, it's been my experience that for change to have a lasting effect, and for it to be considered change rather than reactive change, a step-by-step approach is often more effective. This involves making one small incremental change, and then another, as we move from one area of our life to the next.

This approach allows us to:

- build momentum and confidence;
- consider our options and develop a well-thought-out plan of attack;
- reflect on the changes we're already making before we make another one;

- reduce our stress levels and build our energy levels as we go before we take on bigger challenges;
- learn as we go – for example, what worked, what could have worked better, and what would I do differently next time?

You may find it useful to consider this when deciding which approach to take, and which actions you want to take, when, why and how.

Creating ripples

Here's another approach that I've always found particularly useful.

A ripple effect occurs when one or more areas of your life influence another one. It's a knock-on or domino effect similar to dropping a stone into a calm pool of water. The stone may only hit one area of the water, but the ripples that result from this impact can be seen across a much wider area; and the same can be true in life.

Negative ripples

Let's say I'm feeling unhappy in my work role, but I'm finding it hard to switch off these negative emotions at the end of each day, and my underlying feelings of frustration, stress and disappointment come home with me each night. After a while, these feelings begin to fester away under the surface because I've taken no action to remedy my situation. As they build in intensity, they start to spill over into other areas of my life.

My relationship is beginning to suffer; I've stopped doing regular exercise and I've stopped socializing outside work. When I do go out, I seem to go from one extreme to another and party harder than ever before, behaviour that's only adding to my problems at home.

As time passes and still no action is taken, I'm feeling even more depressed and apathetic regarding life in general. I feel trapped and have no idea how to break the cycle.

Janene

Not only did I have physical and psychological symptoms, but I started to notice the effects that this was having on my personal quality of life and my relationship with my husband. I lost my pleasure for life and used to spend time worrying about the future.

Using the above example (which is a common one), you can see how one unhappy stone hitting the water in the career sector of someone's life can send out a negative ripple across many other areas when no action is taken to remedy or change the situation.

Positive ripples

If you've ever renovated a house, you'll understand the concept of positive ripples only too well. Do you remember how as you completed one room, the rest of the house started to look even more like it needed decorating than it did before you started? Now you have something fresh to compare it to, you're more able to see the cracks in the walls or where the carpet and colour schemes are becoming faded. Before you had completed the other room, every room looked the same, so it wasn't as easy to see the areas that needed to be worked on. But now, it's all suddenly crystal clear and you're wondering why you couldn't see the cracks and faded colours before.

This analogy demonstrates a positive ripple effect – as we make a positive change in one area of our lives, we can become more confident about making new changes in other areas, or we start to notice the indirect positive knock-on effect that those changes have had in other areas.

So, when you're creating your Action Plan, you may want to consider which actions, if taken, could create a positive ripple in other areas of your life at the same time.

This way, you may be able to influence how you feel about another area without actually addressing it as a specific action point, thereby keeping your action points down and your time and energy focused.

Thomas
Burnout for me has been a positive experience. In the end I was forced to drop a lot of things and slow down. That opened up the space for introspection and the chance to see the situation for what it really was.

But what if it doesn't work?

Does the expression 'self-fulfilling prophecy' ring any bells? There's a line in the 1999 *Matrix* film that goes something like this: 'there's a difference between knowing the path, and walking the path'. You've already seen how powerful your internal dialogue can be when it comes to the results you achieve in life. So if there's a negative internal dialogue going on that's full of woe and doubt, deal with it now, because it will only hold you back as you try to move forward.

Work out where it's coming from – a negative past experience perhaps, low confidence or self-esteem, the influence of your clan/tribe – and find a new song to sing. How much you allow this internal assault on your efforts to gain power is completely in your hands.

Part A: What, not how

This approach to your action planning will help you to:

- collate your ROEI ratings for your external world;
- highlight those areas of your life that are going well, look for ways to ensure you maintain this same level of momentum, and help you to see how you can learn from these experiences;
- explore where the positive 'ripples' may exist;
- identify where common themes may exist;
- create your Action Plan;
- prioritize your activities to keep them realistic and achievable;
- identify your motivators for wanting to make change;
- consider ways to keep yourself motivated and inspired;
- start to feel better about your life.

There are four steps to creating your Action Plan. Follow each step and take as much time as you need to consider the questions you're being asked, as your responses to each step will help you to define your final Action Plan.

Step 1: Collating your ROEI ratings

Use the summary table (Table 7.1) provided to collate all of the ROEI ratings that you allocated to each aspect of your external world. This table provides you with a summarized view of how you're currently investing your energy and the rate of return you feel you're getting from that investment. So if you want to change any of your ratings, now's the time to do so.

Note:

For the ROEI 'Family' rating, you can either take the average ROEI across all of the family members you've listed, or you could re-create the table and add in as many additional lines as you need in order to list each family member separately.

Likewise, if you have additional factors that you've considered that were not covered in the book, you may want to re-create Table 7.1 to incorporate these factors.

Now consider the following questions:

- Having completed your ROEI summary, how do you feel about what it is currently telling you?
- Which areas of your life are giving you a great return on your energy investment?
- Which areas are creating the greatest stress/energy depletion for you?

Table 7.1 My ROEI summary

Area of External World	ROEI Ratings		
	1	2	3
Career/work role			
Academic study			
Home aesthetics			
Living environment			
Finances			
Culture (home)			
Culture (immediate workplace)			
Culture (organization)			
Culture (my clan/tribe)			
Personal growth and development			
Professional growth and development			
Relationship			
Social network			
Support network			
Social/recreational activities			
Own behaviour			
Other people's behaviour			
Social conforms			
Family			
Community			

Step 2: What's working well?

Always being one who likes to look on the bright side of life, let's take a moment to explore what's working really well for you at the moment.

List below all of the areas of your external world that you rated as a 3 – that is, above average or maximum energy return on energy invested.

Now consider what all of these areas have in common. For example, are you doing a similar activity, around similar people; working towards a common goal; sharing similar dreams or ambitions; gaining intellectual stimulation; meeting a specific need or motivator? There may be one or several common themes between each of these areas, but understanding why you're currently receiving a good ROEI is important, as this information will tell you a lot about what you may need more of, or what may be missing from other areas of your life. Use the space below to record your thoughts:

What do these common themes tell you about yourself and what energizes you?

What steps can you put in place to make sure you maintain this/these same ROEI rating(s)?

What, if anything, could prevent you from maintaining your desired level of momentum?

What steps can you put in place to help manage this/these situations should they arise?

You'll be referring back to this information later on as you use it to help you in lower ROEI-rated areas of your life.

Step 3: Assessing your energy vampires

In Step 3 we're going to identify where your biggest energy vampires and stress areas lie, and start to fine-tune your span of attention.

List below all of the areas of your external world that you rated as a 2 – that is, a moderate return on energy invested.

Now list all of the areas of your external world that you rated as a 1 – that is, little or no return on energy invested.

What common themes (if any) can you see?

What does this tell you about yourself, what you may need more of, or what you may be missing from these areas of your life?

Now it's time to consider the level of change that may be required in each of these areas in order for you to start getting a better ROEI. Use the following questions to help you to do this:

Which area(s) could start giving you a better return on your energy investment if you made only small changes (e.g. changes that could be completed easily within a month and would help you to build some momentum)?

Which area(s) could start giving you a better return on your energy investment if you made more considered changes (e.g. changes that may require some thought, planning or research, could positively impact on smaller areas of low/moderate ROEI, and could be completed within, say, three months)?

Which area(s) would require more significant changes before you would start to get a better return on your energy investment? (This means changes that may require a more long-term strategy or approach, but would positively impact on several low/moderate ROEI areas of your life and be completed within, say, six months or more.)

Given your answers to the last three questions, how will you prioritize your actions? (That is, where can you create positive ripple effects or what would make the biggest difference to you right now?)

Step 4: Creating your Action Plan

When it comes to planning for change, there's no 'one size fits all' approach that works for everyone. Some people like to tackle their biggest challenge first and then knock off their smaller ones later on (Option A below), while others like to build up to their major change by tackling their smaller challenges first and building up some momentum (Option B).

Your answers to the questions in Step 3 should have started to provide you with a guide as to which approach would suit you best, given your available time, energy and resources.

So, consider which approach you'd like to take and then use the questions below to do a final check that you're on track before you create your Action Plan.

Option A: Tackling your biggest challenge first and then knocking off your smaller ones later

- If changes were made in this area of your life, would it make the greatest impact on how you're currently feeling?
- How important is making this change to you at this time?
- How much energy do you have to invest in making this change?
- If now is not the right time, but you still desire change, when will you make it?
- What difference(s) do you think you'll start to notice in yourself and its related ROEI as you make this change?
- What difference(s) do you want to see in other areas of your life as you make this change (positive ripple effect)?
- What specific activities do you need to do to slay this energy vampire?
- How can you use your knowledge about what's working well for you in your life (ROEI 3 ratings) to help you in your action planning?

- What questions do you need to ask yourself as you prepare to take action?
- How can you find the answers to these questions?
- If you're nervous about tackling this energy vampire, what other information do you need to have to feel more confident about moving forward?
- How can you find this information?
- What else do you need to know at this time?
- Realistically, how long will this change take?
- How will you keep yourself motivated during the change?
- What could prevent you from following through on this change?
- How can you manage this risk/these risks should it/they arise?
- How will you know you're on track to success? (What short-term success milestones can you put in place to maintain your momentum?)
- What could be the long-term consequences for you if you do not make this change?
- How do you think you'll feel once you've completed this change?

Note:

- Once you've answered the questions relating to 'what could prevent you' and 'how can you manage this potential risk', incorporate your risk management strategies into your Action Plan. By being proactive in this area, you'll be well prepared should the event arise.
- Before you complete all of the specific tasks/activities in your Action Plan, why not have a browse through the next chapter to see if anything rings a bell in terms of possible approaches you could take.

Option B: Building up to your big change by tackling your smaller challenges first and developing some momentum

- Which areas of your life would require only small changes in them for you to gain a greater return on your energy investment?
- If these changes were made, how would they impact on your current energy level?
- What positive ripple effect could these changes have on other areas of your life?
- How will you use the momentum you gain from these changes as you approach new challenges?
- If now is not the right time, but you still desire change, when will you make it?
- How important is this change/these changes to you at this time?
- How much energy do you have to invest in making this/these change(s)?

- How long will this/these change(s) take?
- What difference(s) do you think you'll start to notice in yourself and your current ROEI as you make this/these change(s)?
- What difference(s) do you want to see in other areas of your life as you make this/these change(s)?
- What specific activities do you need to do to slay this vampire?
- How can you use your knowledge about what's working well for you in your life (ROEI 3 ratings) to help you in your action planning?
- What questions do you need to ask yourself as you prepare to take action?
- How can you find the answers to these questions?
- As you build up to your larger energy vampires, which ones do you feel will have the greatest impact on how you're currently feeling? (That is, which will you tackle next?)
- Which area will you tackle last?
- How will you prioritize each phase of activity?
- If you're nervous about tackling this/these vampire(s), what other information do you need to have to feel more confident about taking action?
- How can you find this information?
- What else do you need to know at this time?
- How long will this/these change(s) take?
- How will you keep yourself motivated during the changes ahead?
- What could prevent you from following through?
- How can you manage this/these risk(s) should it/they arise?
- How will you know you're on track to success? (That is, what short-term success milestones can you put in place to maintain your momentum?)
- What could be the long-term consequences for you if you do not make this/these change(s)?
- How will you feel once you've completed this/these change(s)?

Note:

- Once you've answered the questions relating to 'what could prevent you' and 'how can you manage this potential risk', incorporate your risk management strategies into your Action Plan. By being proactive in this area, you'll be well prepared should the event arise.
- Before you complete all the specific tasks/activities in your Action Plan, why not have a browse through the next chapter to see if anything rings a bell in terms of possible approaches you could take.

So we come to the end of Part A and your first action-planning phase. How does it feel? Better, I hope, because you're now able to focus your energy on those areas of your external world that will really start to make the biggest difference to your overall ROEI.

As you progress with your Action Plan, you may wish to amend it a little to incorporate new activities as you learn more about this area of the stress/energy equation. If you find yourself doing this, make sure you amend your activity time-frames accordingly if they're likely to be affected by these new activities in any way. Also, remember the general rule of thumb about not taking on too much at once if you do decide to add in some new activities along the way.

Part B: How, not what

Using the Action Plan template at the end of this chapter, this approach to your action planning will help you to:

- evaluate each area of your internal energy reserve;
- identify where common themes may exist;
- create your Action Plan;
- prioritize your activities to keep them realistic and achievable;
- identify your motivators for wanting to make change;
- consider ways to keep yourself motivated and inspired;
- start to feel better about yourself.

This approach is the one that I used to cope with my own burnout, and to work my way out of it. I still use this approach today when I need to recharge a particular aspect of my energy reserve or feel I'm falling a little out of balance, or I need to stretch my energy boundaries a tad to build up an increased energy reserve for an upcoming challenge.

The E-Plan

I've called the approach the 'Energizer Plan' or 'E-Plan' and it has five stages to it:

1 Evaluate: assessing the 'current state' of your energy levels across all three of your internal energy centres.
2 Energize: making changes to address any imbalance and to create balance.
3 Establish: bringing about your new 'normal' – a state of equilibrium when all three of your energy centres are in balance.
4 Extend: learning how to slowly push the boundaries of your new balanced state and to come back to a state of balance again.
5 Elevate: learning how to build spare energy capacity to create an increased energy reserve.

This approach adopts a slow but steady approach to effective energy management, an approach that requires continual observation of yourself as you move through each stage. So you may find it useful to keep a log or journal to record your insights and observations as you go, because from here on in I want you to think of yourself as your very own controlled experiment as you learn about yourself, your energy, and those techniques that re-energize or deplete your energy levels. You'll also be monitoring your external environment and the impacts this may be having on your energy levels as you move through each stage.

To assist you in this task, for each stage of the E-Plan I've provided various activities to help you to keep your finger on the pulse of any changes you experience, as you experience them.

No silver bullet

Before you get started, I'd like to say straight away that there is no silver bullet when it comes to starting to feel energized and engaged with life again. I don't mean this to be patronizing or to depress you; far from it. It just seems that sometimes our 'need for speed' can have a habit of spilling over into our approach to energy management too – we want to feel better and we want it now.

If you truly want to break the cycle of poor energy management and to start feeling a natural level of sustained energy for longer periods of time, then you'll need to take a slower road to the healing process, I'm afraid. Remember, it took a long time to get to how you're feeling now, so it's logical that it will take a while to get you back to feeling more energized again.

It's also important not only to know when to ask yourself questions, but to know when to ask for help too. This book has in no way been designed to replace professional therapy or guidance, so if you need some additional support in your battle to retrieve your lost energy and vitality for life, then please seek out that help and assistance.

By taking responsibility for how you're feeling, the energy you take from others and the energy you send out into the world and to those around you, you place yourself in the empowering position of making changes that will not only impact on how you feel, but how those closest to you feel too.

Time-frame

The time-frame for completing these five steps will vary for each person, depending on where you're currently sitting on the energy imbalance scale at this time. For me, it took around three months to reach stage 3 and to feel 'normal' again. When I say 'normal', I don't mean the normal that I had come to accept before burnout. No, this was a new normal that I had a vague and distant memory of but hadn't experienced for some time. It was a state of balance that spanned across all three of my energy centres and created a renewed sense of calm within.

From there, I was able to start learning how to manage my energy as I pushed my new boundaries and then returned to a state of balance again (stages 4 and 5). Over the months that followed, using this same technique, I was able to learn how to generate energy reserves for times when I would need them the most. This is a technique I still use.

This process may take a shorter or longer period of time for you. There's no right or wrong answers here. This is your journey, so take whatever time you need to take to remain committed and focused on the end result you want to achieve.

OK, now it's time to get your E-Plan underway with step 1: Evaluate.

Step 1: Evaluate – assessing the 'current state' of your energy levels across all three of your energy centres

1A) Assessing your 'current state'

In Chapter 6, you explored each of the energy centres and answered a series of questions for each one. Based on your answers and the signs of imbalance that you may currently be experiencing, use the following scale to rate where you feel your current energy levels are for each aspect of your energy reserve:

1 = very low: you have little or no energy and may feel permanently fatigued for most of the time. You feel you're experiencing many of the more severe symptoms of energy depletion listed.

2 = moderately low: you have some energy early in the day, but find your energy levels declining rapidly by midday when fatigue starts to set in. You could identify with most of the signals of energy depletion and have started to notice the early signs of some of the more severe signals listed.

3 = neutral: your energy levels are neither high nor low, but you find that it doesn't take too much to deplete your energy. You feel you have little energy left in reserve when you need it and could identify with some of the less severe energy depletion signals listed.

4 = moderately high: your energy levels are generally quite good and you have some energy in reserve, but find yourself feeling quite tired at weekends or when you relax. You could identify with a couple of the less severe energy depletion signals listed.

5 = very high: you generally have a high energy level for most of the time and have learnt how to re-energize your energy levels well. You do not feel you're experiencing any of the warning signals listed.

Place your rating for each area under 'Current Energy Rating' in the table provided (Table 7.2). Don't worry about the other two columns at this time ... we're coming to them shortly.

Table 7.2 My energy reserve summary

Energy Centre	Current Energy Rating	Intermediate Energy Rating (Goal 1)	Long-term Energy Rating (Goal 2)
Spiritual energy			
Psychological energy (overall)			
Physical energy			

1B) Intermediate Energy Rating (Goal 1)

Using the same rating scale, given your current energy rating, identify what you feel would be a realistic goal for you, one that could be achieved through consistent action and assessment over a period of, say, three months. (If you want to set your goal for further away than three months, do so – as long as you achieve this critical middle ground before going for the final furlong.)

Depending on where you are now, this could be halfway to moderately/very high, or all the way to very high for you, but make sure your first goal is achievable given where you are now. If you set the goal too high and overestimate your ability to achieve it, you're only setting yourself up to fail, which is not only a waste of valuable energy, but self-defeating too. So be honest and err on the side of caution if you're unsure. It's better to aim and shoot beyond your goal than to miss it altogether.

If you need some help with this one, take a look at the Quick Tips below before making your assessment.

Place this new goal rating in the Intermediate Energy Rating (Goal 1) column in Table 7.2.

Quick Tips:
If you rated your current energy levels for each area as being 3 or below, then your intermediate goal may be to achieve your new 'normal' state

of energy balance in three months' time – perhaps stage 3, which is a sensible and achievable goal for you to aim for.

If you rated your current energy levels as being either moderately high or very high (4 or 5), then your three-month goal might be very different for you or you may not have one at all.

1C) Long-term Energy Rating (Goal 2)

Now think ahead to when you've achieved your first energy goal (Goal 1) in, let's say, three months' time. What do you want your energy ratings to look like in six or nine months' time (i.e. six to nine months after you've achieved your first goal)?

Place this new rating in the Long-term Energy Rating (Goal 2) column in Table 7.2.

Note:

It may seem a little strange to ask you to complete your three- and six-month energy goals while you're assessing your current state and before you've had an opportunity to see exactly what's involved in completing your E-Plan. However, there is a cunning plan behind this approach.

As you enter into your E-Plan activities, it's important to have the right mindset, one that wants to commit to creating change. There's no better way of doing this than to be realistic about where you're currently at, and then to work out where you want to be. If you already have the motivation to initiate change, then all you're providing yourself with is a sensible target to aim for.

It's a bit like joining a weight loss club. Right at the beginning you'll weigh in and establish your ideal weight and goal. Everything you do in the interim is then tailored towards you achieving that goal. I've adopted the same approach here as it prevents us from wandering around in an endless wilderness pursuing a nameless goal, because you now know what you're aiming for.

However, like all goals, these targets are also flexible; so if you find as you progress with your E-Plan that you want to amend your target ratings or associated activities, then please do so. This is your plan, so take control of it and customize it to meet your needs.

Step 2: Energize – making changes to address imbalance and to create balance

In Step 2, you'll be identifying actions that will help you towards achieving your first energy goal: Intermediate Energy Rating (Goal 1). You may stay in this stage of your E-Plan for a month, two, three months or longer depending on the rating that you gave your current energy level(s).

If you find you need an extra month or so to complete this goal, then that's fine. As mentioned earlier, tailor your E-Plan to fit your needs, not the other way round. The objective is that you make it to your first goal intact, not with a lower energy level than you started with.

2A) Making changes

OK, you've established your current state and you've identified your desired intermediate goal. Now you need to consider the 'how' part – that is, what specific activities do you either need to increase, implement or reduce in order to achieve your first goal?

If you need some help with the 'how am I going to get there' bit, why not:

- review your responses to the Energy Pulse Check questions in Chapter 6. Are there any insights to be gained there?
- take a look at some of the questions listed for Options A and B in Part A of this chapter to see if anything triggers an idea;
- have a browse through the following chapter to see if anything flicks your switch in there too;
- consider which area(s) of action would give you the greatest positive ripple effect(s);
- consider staggering your activities over your allotted time-frame for Goal 1 to build up momentum as your energy starts to become more balanced;
- focus on one energy centre at a time and build up your momentum.

Capture your initial thoughts in the space below:

It's important to consider your risk management plan too. In other words, what could prevent you from following through on the actions you've listed and how will you manage this/these events should they occur? Now go to the end of this chapter and complete your Action Plan along with any associated risks you'll be managing as well. Then continue with the next section, 'Monitoring your progress'.

2B) Monitoring your progress

Now it's time to consider how you'll adopt the role of the impartial observer as you progress with this first phase of your Action Plan. By monitoring yourself on a daily basis, you can make notes about how your energy is feeling and why. For example:

- How does each energy centre feel at the end of the day (or the centre you're focusing on)?
- What has affected the energy centre(s) that feel lower that day and why?
- If something detracted from your energy that day, how much did it detract your energy by and for how long?
- Does this happen all the time or only occasionally?
- What approaches worked well to address the immediate imbalance?
- Have you noticed this/these effect(s) on your energy level(s) before, or has it only just come to light?
- Which re-energizing techniques aren't working as well for you and why?
- What elements of your external world seem to affect you the most?
- How long did each approach take before you started to feel the benefits?
- How long did the benefits last and what affected them again?

People often comment that this process feels a little foreign to them when they first start doing it, and it probably will for you too. But trust me when I tell you that, first, once you've played the role of being your own observer for a while, it will soon become second nature; and that, second, you're gathering information now that you'll be able to use not only in the second phase of your E-Plan, but for the rest of your life too. So it's worth the extra effort in the long run.

To assist you in your ongoing monitoring, Table 7.3 gives some possible questions and tips to guide you over the coming months.

Over the coming months, all this information will give you a toolkit of energizing techniques that will enable you to maintain your energy levels regardless of what is going on around you. You'll get to know yourself and your energy centres so well that you'll know exactly how you're feeling, why, and which techniques you need to put in place to re-energize yourself at that time. Now isn't that worth hanging in there for?

Table 7.3 Monitoring your progress: questions and tips

Energy Status	Questions/Tips
If you're experiencing an energy high	• What happened to help me feel this way? • What energizing techniques have I been using lately? OR, What have I not been doing to feel this way? • What benefits am I noticing as a result of these techniques? • How long did it take before I felt this way? • How long are the benefits lasting? • When my energy high lowers, to what level does it go? (That is, does it plummet to an all-time low or reduce to neutral?) • How long has it been since I last felt like this? • How will I know when my energy reserve is running low again? • What have I learnt that I can use when it does start to run a little low again?
If you're experiencing an energy low	You can learn from your energy lows in the same way as you can learn from your energy highs by asking yourself the same set of questions when you feel in need of a recharge.
If you're experiencing a 'neutral energy'	When we take our neutral energy modes for granted, we're missing out on a great opportunity to learn new techniques that will help us to recharge our physical energy before we reach an energy low, thereby adopting a more proactive approach to stress/energy management. We can also explore why we may not have been able to get our levels any higher. To learn more from your neutral energy modes, try asking yourself questions such as: • How long have I felt like this? • When was the last time I felt energized? • When was the last time I had low energy? • What have I been doing in between these times? • What technique would top up my energy level? • How long is my neutral mode lasting? • What happens after this? (That is, is it going down or up again?) • How will I know when my energy reserve is running low? • Do I have enough energy in reserve for upcoming energy demands? • How can I boost my energy to start feeling more energized now? • What can I learn from this?

Step 3: Establish – bringing about your 'new normal', a state of equilibrium when all three of your energy centres are in balance

If you're about to move on to step 3, then you've succeeded in your first energy goal and have achieved your 'new normal'. Well done! The hardest part is now behind you. So how does it feel? Pretty good, I'd imagine. I know it did for me.

By now you should be experiencing:

- feeling more energized for longer periods of time;
- feeling less stressed;
- a growing sense of inner calm;
- feeling more internally balanced or centred;
- a reduction in your original warning signals;
- a reduction in your chemical energy enhancers;
- a greater awareness of yourself and your energy levels;
- the benefits of having a great toolkit of E-Plan energizers;
- feeling more engaged with yourself and life in general again.

3A) Your energy-testing phase

Step 3 is all about learning to maintain this new-found state of inner equilibrium for a period of time, as you interact with your external world. It's your test phase, if you like, when you're able to go about your day-to-day life and deal with unexpected events that would normally drain your energy reserves. This time, though, you're able to bring the balance back quickly and easily using your E-Plan energizer toolkit.

So for this step, I recommend that you remain here for at least one month to six weeks, to ensure you have truly mastered the art of energy rebalancing before you start to experiment by pushing beyond your new boundaries (in step 4).

Keep monitoring your progress, and if you need more or less time in this step, adapt and move on to step 4 when you're ready and not before.

Step 4: Extend – learning how to slowly push the boundaries of your new balanced state and to come back to a state of balance again

By now, you're hopefully feeling the benefits of living with a more balanced internal world and you've tested your new-found energy reserve with various scenarios from your day-to-day life (and some you didn't plan for); and you've also managed to recover your equilibrium quickly and easily.

In step 4, we start to push the boundaries deliberately, by creating small but challenging scenarios that will extend your energy levels beyond the tests they've already survived. We continue this process in step 5 as you learn how to create your energy reserve.

Think of this step as being similar to building a muscle. In the early days we know that we're going to experience some pain as our muscle gets used to being exercised, and our only goal is just to be able to complete the exercises and get up the next day without feeling like we've gone ten rounds with a world heavyweight. After a while, though, as our muscle gets stronger, we need to increase the weight we're using or change our routine to create a stronger muscle; if we don't, we plateau, our muscle gets bored, and our exercise becomes less efficient.

In this example, your energy is your muscle, and step 4 is going to help you to build a stronger energy muscle. Benefits of this step include:

- the beginnings of creating reserve capacity;
- development of new techniques (as required) to address imbalance;
- learning how to address imbalance following times of prolonged energy depletion;
- exploring your new boundaries which are now being extended from your 'new normal' as opposed to where you were several months ago.

Like our muscle, our energy will benefit from small incremental increases in levels of challenge that will build and stretch it slowly, rather than taking on one huge challenge that could put it out of action for a while (and undo all your hard work). So choose your challenges carefully, and make sure they will challenge you progressively, rather than ones that might push you too far, too soon.

The idea is to extend beyond your boundary in a small way and then return to your balanced state using the rebalancing/energizing techniques. Then you'll extend a little further the next time, and then return once again to your balanced state and so on. Each time you will be pushing just a little bit further than before, and each time learning how long it takes you to recover your balance, what techniques worked and when. This is how you start to build your energy reserve.

I stayed in this stage of the E-Plan for another month, so by now I was five months on from my initial experience of burnout. Although I was gaining in strength across my energy centres, I was also wary of becoming over-confident and putting my foot down on the accelerator too hard, too fast and too soon, only to fall back further than I was when I started this step. So as with step 3, I would recommend spending around the same time (one month to six weeks) in this space.

4A) Extending beyond

There are a number of ways you may decide to challenge yourself. For example, you could:

- create a scenario that in the past you've found quite energy depleting just to see how you respond to it now;
- decide to push your normal energy output a little further for a couple of days longer to see how it feels, and to discover when you need to jump back in and re-energize again;
- take on some additional short-term activities to see how they impact on your energy expenditure and recovery process;
- bring an energetic hobby, community project/activity or sport into your life that you may have reduced your commitment to until now.

Each of you will be able to think of scenarios that you know will challenge and stretch your boundaries a little beyond their current energy level, in small and incremental ways. Create a list of these various activities below and work your way through them over the next month to six weeks.

The key to effective energy management is not only to learn how to live in a natural state of balance on a day-to-day basis, but to be able to cope with those inevitable events that life can throw at us, and to be able to return to our state of balance easily and quickly; this is the focus of step 4.

4B) Monitoring your progress

During step 4 continue to monitor your progress. Learn what works for you; what feels too much of a push and why; what techniques are working well for you and for how long; how long it takes you to recover from each new challenge; and how you feel in between and during these challenges.

All the information and insights you're continuing to gain through this step are only adding to what is fast becoming a vast resource at your disposal that will help you to sustain your energy levels from this day forward. No information or knowledge is ever wasted.

Step 5: Elevate – learning how to build enough spare energy capacity to create an energy reserve

By the time you've reached this final step in your E-Plan you're probably starting to feel pretty unstoppable. You're feeling more energized and happy than you've felt in ages and you know more about yourself and your energy levels than you ever thought possible. You've tested and stretched your boundaries, and by now you may even have started scheduling your days and weeks around these natural peaks and troughs in your energy, knowing with a new-found peace of mind that you can recover your energy balance any time you need to.

Now it's time to take all these insights about yourself and start to build your energy reserve, which, through step 4, you've already started to do.

Going back to our muscle analogy, by stretching and recovering your energy levels on a regular basis, like a muscle, you've actually been building your energy's strength, stamina and flexibility all along. You may not need all this strength, stamina and flexibility every day, but at least now you know it's there if you need to tap into it.

By now, you're able to move between states of imbalance and balance easily, but, like our muscles, if we become complacent once we achieve our desired goal, we can start to undo all of the great work we've put in.

5A) Maintenance

Achieving a great state of energy balance is not the end of the process – it's just the beginning but, this time, a new beginning. The new beginning is the rest of your life, and your role is to continue to play the observer in this ongoing process.

Step 5 is your ongoing energy maintenance and monitoring step, where you occasionally (but regularly enough to make a difference) stretch your boundaries to a new level and/or re-test your existing ones.

By staying on top of your energy game, you'll be able to monitor any subtle shifts in your energy, make sure you're not letting things slide, and gain new insights into yourself and how your energy is responding to your external world and its various stressors.

You'll also continue to build your energy reserve, so when an event comes along that demands a great deal of energy from you for a long period of time, you'll not only have the peace of mind that you have the reserve available, you'll know that you also have the tools in place to recover your balance again afterwards. Now that's what I call peace of mind. How about you?

MY ACTION PLAN

Area of Action	Why I Want to Take Action	Specific Task/Activities Required	By When	Review Date

8

Ideas and techniques

When I experienced burnout I was lucky; I had the understanding, knowledge and tools at hand to make the changes I needed to make in my life. So, a nice way to finish might be to share some of these with you where I felt they could add value over and above the work that you've already done. I hope you find them useful.

Recognizing stress

Professional help

If you feel you're experiencing any of the stress-related symptoms detailed in this book, always consider seeking professional help should you feel you want to.

There are many services available both within the workplace in the form of employee assistance programmes, and externally in the form of medical assistance, counselling or coaching. These people are trained to help you, so take advantage of these services. There's no shame in what you're experiencing, so don't feel embarrassed or concerned. It takes more courage to put your hand up and ask for help than it does to hide away.

Support network

Do also tap into your support network. You'll probably find people are more understanding than you may be giving them credit for, and you'll know who these people are. Go to those you feel comfortable with and let them give you the same gift of support, understanding and compassion that you enjoy giving to them.

Recognizing the warning signs and triggers

As you get to know yourself and how you respond to stress, you'll be able to spot when the warning signs are starting to show themselves again. So stay alert and take action immediately to address the imbalance rather than letting them build up. Also, identify your stress triggers and keep a watchful eye over yourself at these times. Pay attention to the trigger, but focus your attention on your response(s) and use the

Some common recovery techniques mentioned in interviews included:

- Exercise
- Better/more sleep
- Improved nutrition/diet
- Massage
- Reiki
- Meditation
- Better time/activity management
- Walking
- Goal-setting/goal-planning
- Vitamin supplements
- Prescribed medication
- Counselling/coaching
- Social and support networks
- Reducing workloads
- 'Work from home' days
- Music (playing/listening)
- Reading
- Confidence-building courses
- Assertiveness skill-building
- Taking leave
- Delegating more
- Taking regular holidays/breaks
- Increased 'me' time
- Building knowledge base.

methods discussed in the book to objectively analyse what's happening to you and how you're feeling. Then use what you learn about yourself to your advantage.

Action planning and decision-making

Taking action

As a coach, my role isn't to come up with all of the answers for my clients; it's to ask the right questions to help them find the right answers for themselves. It may not feel like it right now, but trust me when I say that you do have all of the answers you need inside you to find some form of resolution to the challenges you're currently facing. We all do; it's just that sometimes we can bury them so deep behind a wall of baggage that we can't see them any more.

Throughout the book I've tried to ask you some of the 'right questions' to get you thinking about what action you could take to move things forward. Only you know where things are at for you in your life; how you're feeling; what could prevent you from moving forward; and what needs to happen to overcome these barriers. But the important thing to remember here is that this current stage of your life is the result of choices and decisions you've made in the past. This means that from today you have an opportunity to re-create your life and who you want to be based on the decisions and choices you make from this day forward. All you need to decide is what, when, why and how that will happen.

The tools you use to make these changes will also vary, depending on your specific needs. So use the questions in the book to guide you, access the information you need to decide on the changes you want to make, and then initiate your plan of action. But, above all else, *believe*. Believe in yourself, and believe that anything is possible, with time, focus, patience and commitment.

Trying a different perspective

This is a good one to use if you're having trouble making your mind up about something and you have a little time to decide.

When we make a decision about something, we often experience a psychological or emotional response to that decision. So, let's say you have two options to choose from. Imagine for a while that you've made the decision to go with option one and stay with that decision long enough to send the right signals to your brain that you have actually made that decision (because your mind only knows what you tell it to be true, rather than the reality of a situation). Then stick with the decision for 24 or 48 hours. How do you feel? What emotions are you experiencing? What is your gut telling you? Then repeat the process for your second option.

Use the responses you experience for each decision as indicators as to how you would actually feel if you had just made that decision. It may sound like a strange approach, but it does work.

James
I keep my work and personal life quite separate now and I've got better at seeing problems on the horizon and at proactively tackling them head on. I have a day of complete relaxation once a week and I pull back

straight away if I notice my energy is flagging. I also do active meditation when I'm walking.

Viewing yourself as someone else

Sometimes we're great at giving advice to others, but how often have you thought to yourself, 'I should be listening to my own advice!' That's what viewing you as someone else is all about. Ask yourself, if this were happening to someone else and they asked my advice, what would I say and what questions would I ask?

It's another great way of emotionally detaching from your own situation and taking a more objective view of it.

Procrastination

Procrastination may be the thief of time, but in my experience it's also used as an excuse not to take action. People often say 'Oh, I procrastinate a lot' to explain why they haven't taken action, but procrastination is only a symptom, not a cause. Work out what's going on beneath the surface for you and why you're not moving forward, and make that your focus of attention.

Time wasting

What are you doing that you don't really need to be doing? Explore areas of your life and work that you could be delegating to others, and if you have problems trusting others, identify what you need to do to learn how to let go – for example, weekly updates, or other forms of regular communication.

Learning to say no

When we have trouble saying no to people it's often because deep down we want everyone to be happy, or we're a born people-pleaser. Either way, we're often only making a rod for our own backs as we take on more and more with little or no regard for ourselves. Learning to say no in an assertive way doesn't actually mean saying no completely to everyone, it just means saying no to doing it right now. Just think of a time when someone has said no to you in a polite but helpful way. I bet you didn't mind one bit, did you? So why not try taking this approach on board yourself?

Get organized

Nothing creates a more fertile breeding ground for stress than disorganization. So why not review your personal and professional life and look for opportunities to start bringing some routine into your life? The more organized you are, the more efficient you'll be; and the more efficient you are, the less stressed you'll be.

Mary
My confidence is building again slowly, but burnout taught me how to spot the warning signs in advance and to focus my mind on more proactive planning now.

Celebrate the small wins

Remember to celebrate the small wins along the way. These are the things that keep you motivated and help you to see the progress you're making. I celebrated my small wins all the way during my own recovery from burnout and they made a huge difference to me psychologically and emotionally. They don't have to be huge gestures. Perhaps a massage, a new CD or book, or a day trip somewhere.

What's worked before?

This is a short one. What approaches to change, stress or energy management have you used in the past that you can implement now?

Blind spots

Have you noticed how good we are at spotting other people's blind spots, but how poor (or unwilling) we can be at owning up to our own? It takes courage to gaze into the eyes of our blind spots. We all know they exist, but I guess as long as we think we can't see them, we figure they can't see us either. If you suspect you might have a few when it comes to some areas of your life, why not ask a trusted friend to give you some constructive feedback on the topic. Alternatively, find yourself a coach or someone similar who may be able to help you to unearth whatever might be hiding in your blind spot(s).

Being congruent

When we're finding it hard to achieve a certain goal, it can often be because we're not being congruent in our thoughts, words and actions. For example, we may be saying and doing all the right things, but we don't actually believe we can achieve our goal. So if you have a trail of failed goals behind you, and they've all been realistically achievable, it might be worth exploring how congruent you've been in the past and how you can turn that knowledge about yourself around to work in your favour this time.

Energy vampires

If your energy vampires are environmental or situational – such as your job, finances, living environment, academic studies – start by using your answers to each of these sections in the book to consider possible ways of making changes. Then all you need to decide is what's within your scope of control to change, when and how.

If your energy vampires are of a more social nature, such as friends or work colleagues, here are some tips you might find useful.

Mitchell
I took some time off and started on a rehab programme, small regular meals and participating in gentle exercise at regular intervals. Then I started looking for a new job.

Throwing the baton

If you're unable to remove this person from the equation altogether, you need to start protecting yourself. Remember the more you keep supplying the energy fix, the more they'll just keep coming back to you. So you've got to learn to be polite but assertive with them, stop trying to fix their problems for them, and start helping them to help themselves.

For example, you could say something like 'I can see you're upset about this. What's one thing you could do to make a difference to how you're feeling right now?'

The more you keep throwing the baton back to your energy vampires, the more you'll teach them new behaviour when it comes to how they interact with you. They'll either start adapting their own behaviour accordingly or they'll get bored and move on. Either way, they're no longer your problem and you've survived with your energy intact.

Shields up

A good visual technique I've used on many occasions is to imagine a protective bubble around me whenever I'm around new energy vampires. Visualize all their negative energy just bouncing right off your protective shield and right back at them. Use this with the above technique and you'll be surprised how quickly they'll start to disappear. Why? Because they can sense that you're no longer engaging in the game.

Stress/energy management

Increase your knowledge bank

Increase your knowledge bank when it comes to understanding what you're experiencing and why – for example, how your body functions under stress, how various symptoms can manifest, etc. Use the wealth of information that's available to you on stress and stress management, because the more you learn, the more you'll take the mystery out of the equation and defuse any fears or concerns you may have.

Mini micro-charging

Find ways to do mini micro-charges during the day and bring those into your life too. For example, a quick walk around the block, stretching at your desk, or taking regular mini-breaks when you're supposed to at work. Micro-charging techniques are just as important as the ones that require more time and effort.

Get into your rhythm

Everyone has a natural rhythm; some people are night owls and others are early birds. Identify your own natural rhythm and use it to schedule your day. For example, if you know that your natural peak is between 7 a.m. and 3 p.m., try devoting this time to your more challenging activities and keep your administrative activities for later in the day.

Another good tip for extending your natural peak time is to use one of your energy recharging techniques about two hours before your energy starts to wane. You'll notice that you're able to stay more alert and engaged for longer this way.

'Journalling'

'Journalling' is a great way to empty our minds and quietly externalize what's going on inside. It can also help us to find solutions to our problems at the same time.

Bethany
I took some time off work for a while and then increased my down time; I sought professional help and took medication for a while too and undertook counselling. I also had great support from my family and learnt that I could recover my sense of achievement and belief in myself again.

Career or work role

This is potentially a huge topic, so I'm going to narrow it down a little.

Available resources

Use the resources that are available to you (i.e. books on effective career planning, career counsellors or coaches, your manager, mentors, role models, etc.). Utilize these resources to get clear about exactly why you're unhappy, what you want from your work/career, and what needs to change.

Mind mapping

Try mind mapping your current and last two work roles. To do this, draw a mind map identifying all of the aspects of your role that you enjoy and why (what needs does it meet for you – that is, a sense of achievement, making a difference, etc.).

Then do another for all of the aspects that you don't enjoy and why.

Your 'whats' will give you a list of essential elements that you need to be happy in your work and those that you may need to avoid in future roles, and your 'whys' will give you a glimpse at what you value about your work (over and above remuneration, which is a given) and what motivates you.

Then explore new ways of packaging the aspects you love about your work into different roles or career paths.

Replacing fiction with fact

Make research your new best friend. Often we make career decisions based on perception rather than reality. What do you need to know about making a career or role change and how and where can you find this information?

One of the best ways of conducting research that I always recommend is through informational interviews (talking to people who are doing what you'd like to do). They're not the same as networking, because you're not asking for a job, you're only gathering information, and you'll find most people receptive to the idea of sharing what they know.

Develop a transition plan

Remember that you don't have to make your career change right now if you're unable or not ready to. So long as you're clear about where you want to end up and have a plan of action to get there, how long it takes to arrive is up to you.

Personal and professional growth and development

As well as the ideas discussed in Chapter 5 for personal development, here are a few more to consider.

Adam
I prioritize my work now and don't go on guilt trips any more if I say no to someone. I've also learnt to relax more than I ever did before and take regular time out for myself too, as well as making more time for recreational activities and other people, which really energizes me.

Who do you want to be?

If I asked you to describe your 'idealized self', what would you say? How would you describe yourself? What do you look like? How do you act? What characteristics do you have? What is your life like? What are your friends like?

What changes do you need to make to bridge the gap between where you are now and where you want to be?

Rewriting your programming

If you'd like to work on rewriting some of your negative internal chatter about yourself or how you view other people, then here's a great technique that I've recommended many times:

- Identify any triggers that set off this negative internal dialogue – for example, when asked to do public speaking.
- Monitor what you're saying to yourself when these situations arise, such as, 'I'm useless at public speaking'.
- Identify the origins of this internal chatter and ask yourself if it's still relevant for you. For example, 'Bad past experience at the age of six ... um ... no.'
- If it isn't, write yourself a new song to sing that you can put in place each time one of these triggers appears. For example, 'I'm great at public speaking and find it really energizing' (fake it till you make it).
- Use reminders to keep your new song present in your mind. For example, a note in your diary or written on something else that you see every day.
- When one of these situations arises, press the pause button in your mind, take a deep breath, and repeat your new mantra to yourself as you take action.

Each time you do this, you're sending a message to your brain that there is more than one 'file' available for it to access. With consistent application, your brain will eventually stop looking for the old file and will only access the new one.

With regard to faking it till you make it: in the beginning, your internal critic will be saying things like, 'Oh, you're hopeless at public speaking.' Just ignore it and it'll get bored and go away eventually.

Windows of reality

We've already seen how damaging negative internal chatter can be. If you keep telling yourself that you can't do something, or that something is impossible, then your brain will accept it as being true, and will support you all the way by providing you with the evidence you need to back up your belief system.

You are in charge of the reality you choose to accept. No one else creates your reality for you. This is the window through which you have chosen to view yourself, and the world around you. So it can be a healthy exercise sometimes to ask yourself, 'Is this actually my reality, or is this what I've chosen to believe?' If you're honest with yourself when you answer, you might be surprised at what new opportunities for change can come to light.

Sean
I'm continually alert for the signs and symptoms of when I'm starting to feel overloaded now, so I'm more able to slam the brakes on and stop things from taking a wrong turn again towards burnout.

Circles of influence

We often create stress for ourselves by trying to change things that are outside our scope of control. Work with what's within your scope of control, or those aspects that you have some ability to influence. This way you'll reduce your stress levels and focus your energy more effectively.

The rocking chair

This is a good exercise to use as a reality check.

Close your eyes and imagine yourself at 80, sitting in a rocking chair in your garden. You're looking back on your life and reflecting on all of the many experiences you've had. What will be the things about your life that you'll regret the most?

Emotional addiction

Yes, you can become addicted to your emotions, or at least the chemicals that create those emotional responses – for example, the excitement and increased energy you can experience when adrenaline is pumping around your system and you feel like a three-year-old on a sugar high.

When we're under continual stress, we can become accustomed to our extra shots of adrenaline and cortisol to get us through the day, and we start to enjoy the heightened states that they produce.

However, like all forms of chemical addiction, it isn't long before the usual fix that our body supplies is no longer enough, so we start to seek out new ways of getting our fix – for example, creating new dramas in our lives, indulging in self-sabotaging behaviours, or in other adrenaline-pumping activities such as extreme sports and increased high-energy workouts.

The danger with this approach, however, is that if we're already under stress (which is why we have so much adrenaline and cortisol pumping around our systems in the first place), our minds/bodies are already under pressure, so when we engage in additional activities to increase our supply, we can end up actually causing ourselves more damage in the long run.

So if you've noticed recurring periods of excessive stress in your life, why not consider whether emotional addiction could be playing a role in this repeated behavioural pattern, why that might be, and whether there are other ways you could achieve the emotional high without the repeated stress.

Behaviour

Your own behaviour

For tips on refining aspects of your own behaviour, see the sections under 'Personal and professional growth and development' (page 110) for more on this topic.

Other people's behaviour (includes the clan/tribe)

Other people's behaviour definitely falls outside your scope of control. What you can control, however, is how you respond to that behaviour (note the use of the word 'respond', rather than the word 'react'), so use that as your base from which to work.

First review your responses to the questions on page 50 in the book and then check out the suggestions under 'Energy vampires' (page 107) and 'Personal and professional growth and development' (page 110) in this chapter for further ideas.

Another useful tip is to view other people's behaviour that we find upsetting from an analytical, rather than an emotional, perspective. Remember the sections on how behaviour manifests into actions and results, and how we're only able to see around 10 per cent of the equation when it comes to other people's behaviour? Make what might be going on underneath the surface your focus if you feel the relationship is worth your time and energy, rather than focusing on the behaviour itself.

Donna
People and things just don't wind me up like they used to. I can see the games people play and I choose not to engage. I've surrounded myself with amazing people and have vanquished all of my vampires. Life rocks!

Spiritual energy

Meditation

Meditation is a great way to get out of your own head and into a stress-free zone for a while.

When we meditate on a regular basis we enhance our ability to relax and to create a much needed inner calm and peace that helps us to balance the energy equation, and our overall energy reserve.

I find active meditation while walking or just quiet meditation time in nature works for me, and it's now a part of my life that I'll never be without.

There are many books, tapes and CDs available to guide you through the various meditation techniques. For example, the use of mantras, active meditation, or listening to CDs with music and a voice that guides you through the process.

Regular meditation in an already busy life requires discipline, but the benefits we gain from this simple technique more than pay us back for our time investment. So my advice is to explore the various techniques available and try a few on until you find one that's just your size.

Reiki, etc.

There are now a number of gentle re-energizing techniques available to us (e.g. Reiki, Tai Chi, Shiatsu, Yoga, etc.). Some of these provide gentle exercise as well as ways of learning how to create inner balance;

and some focus purely on rebalancing your internal energy (chakras). They complement all other forms of exercise and provide you with an opportunity to switch out and slow yourself down for a while.

Massage

We all know that massage is a great way to get the knots out of our poor tensed-up muscles, but we can also benefit from the emotional and psychological gains of healing touch, and from the quiet and relaxing space that massage creates for us.

Psychological energy

An attitude of gratitude

Sometimes, when we're feeling a little overwhelmed by life, we only seem to focus on the things that seem to be going wrong; and once we're in this mood, it can be hard to shift ourselves out of it.

If we want to bring this downward spiral to a grinding halt, a good way to do it is to start thinking about all of the things we have in our lives that are going well, that we're grateful for, that we love, and that make us happy. Remember, your emotional responses are the direct result of what's going on in your editing room, so to change how you're feeling, you need to change the internal reel of film and play a different movie. It's almost impossible to stay in a negative mood when we're thinking about things that make us happy or make us laugh. It's just not chemically possible.

Coping mechanisms

Remember the stress model in Chapter 1? Well, your coping mechanisms kick in somewhere between you experiencing pressure and then choosing to respond to it (stress reaction). Our coping mechanisms are usually based on our past experiences and conditioning and they're fundamental when it comes to how effectively we're able to respond to, and work through stress in our lives, and ultimately how we manage our energy levels.

So if you suspect that your in-built stress response unit could do with an upgrade, this is definitely an area that I would recommend that you explore further.

There are many resources available through stress counsellors, books, and on-line materials that can help you to assess your own coping mechanisms and find where areas for improvement may lie.

Distract yourself

Sometimes doing something completely different can help to distract your mind – for example, crosswords, housework, gardening, creative hobbies, reading a book, etc. When we engage in these activities we give our brains something else to think about and the space to come up with solutions.

Do something for someone else

This is a short one. Nothing can take our minds off our own troubles faster than helping someone else through theirs. It seems to put things into perspective for us and gives us a point of focus other than ourselves.

Letting go

Learning to let go of bad experiences is something that should be on every school curriculum. We carry far too much rubbish around in our heads and hearts. We all have bad experiences in life, but what we often fail to do is to learn from them and let them go. Carrying around lots of pent-up anger, frustration, guilt and blame is not only a waste of time and energy, it's no good for your health either.

So if you've got a thorn or two sticking in your side, work out what you need to do, say or think to let it go, and then do yourself a favour and move on. Once you've mastered this technique, pass it on to the next generation. They'll thank you for it when they're older.

Keeping your perspective

We've all had one of those days, when through absolutely no fault of our own one thing after another seems to go awry. The cat throws up on the carpet, you throw up on the cat, and you're fresh out of carpet cleaner and antacids.

Keeping your sense of humour during these times is essential, and so is keeping your perspective. Try not to get an attack of 'molehill and mountain-itis' and end up blowing things out of proportion. Remember to take a step back, take a deep breath, and look at what's happening around you from an objective, rather than emotional, viewpoint. If you really believe, however, that kicking the cat is the only way to feel you've had some form of retribution and regained some control, then find a healthy way to vent your feelings and leave the cat alone. It'll probably only throw up again on the carpet anyway.

Law of attraction

This isn't about affairs of the heart, it's about getting back in life what you focus on. For example, have you ever noticed how people who generally expect bad things to happen to them usually get their wish? This is the law of attraction in action and it works something like this.

As discussed, most of the time we're walking around on automatic pilot, constantly reacting to what's happening around us as our minds actively seek out more of the same to prove our belief systems right.

The law of attraction is about learning to focus your energy only on the things that you want to achieve in life and letting go of any thoughts that will sabotage your efforts. It's like self-fulfilling prophecy and positive thinking rolled into one. The upside being of course that when we only focus on what we want to create, we're more likely to spot the opportunities when they turn up and less likely to sabotage ourselves along the way.

Have fun!

Make a list of all of the things that make you happy and promise yourself to do one every day. These don't need to be time-consuming activities. For many people it can be things as simple as a walk in the park, watching a sunset, taking the dog for a walk, or playing with their children. When we find ways to release our inner-child, we learn to stop taking ourselves so seriously. And you never know, you might actually have some fun along the way too!

Thomas

Accepting the problem and taking action to change it, rather than just trying to cope with it, probably helped me the most. Also, talking to my coach and starting Reiki, because they both create a space for reflection.

Physical energy

Exercise

There are a number of ways that you can learn to manage your physical energy more effectively depending on what you need (i.e. to re-energize or use up your physical energy). Start by using your responses to the questions for this area as your guide and then select those physical activities that you feel will assist you in your Action Plan.

But remember, if you're suffering from excessive stress/burnout, this energy reserve has probably taken quite a pounding, so be mindful of this when you choose your activities, and take it slowly.

Therefore take a considered look at where you are now for this energy centre and design a programme of physical rehabilitation that is progressive and not too demanding.

Diet and nutrition

It goes without saying (but I'll say it anyway) that it doesn't matter what changes you make in your life, if you're still ignoring the basics of good old-fashioned nutrition and diet, you'll be moving one step forward and three steps back. You need fuel; it's that simple.

Adequate sleep

Do I really need to say anything about this one? Thought not!

Cultural

Organizational culture

As an entire organization's culture may fall outside of your scope of control, aim for what you *can* control: your immediate work environment. You can choose how you want to be treated and how you treat other people. You don't have to throw the baby out with the bathwater and give up because you're unable to change the whole organization's culture. Just focus on your little bit of it.

Home culture

Culture is all about behaviour: our own and other people's. So use the tips discussed already and your responses to the questions provided to guide your actions in this area.

Re-establish the rules of engagement, and make sure everyone knows what they are and why. And remember to reward positive behaviours and ignore negative ones, because, as we know, when we pay attention to negative behaviours we're still reinforcing those behaviours.

Danielle

I value my friends more now and endeavour to make time for them. I also had counselling to help me deal with my relationship with my ex in a healthier way. I have down time at weekends and am now looking at changing direction in my career so I can give myself, and my community, more time.

Clan/tribe

Use the questions for this area in the book to identify your who's, what's, why's and how's and then refer to the techniques already provided to guide your areas of action around your own and/or other people's behaviour.

Social and recreational activities

Our social and recreational activities provide us with a great opportunity to recharge ourselves, as long as we're not using them to hype up our adrenaline fix.

Review the previous sections on physical, psychological and spiritual energy and then tailor your recreational activities to meet your needs. But remember, if you haven't done anything remotely resembling exercise for a while, take it easy. I'd hate to lose you this early in the game.

Social and support networks

Use your responses to the questions provided to guide your actions in this area too. Remember that like attracts like, so start to notice how the people around you change as you do. Your current social support network has arrived in your life as a direct response to who you are at this time and what you're projecting out into the world. So doesn't it stand to reason that if you start sending out a different signal, this new frequency will start to attract a different sort of person into your life?

Donna

My support network was amazing during my recovery. They maintained my privacy, never judged me, and were there for me 100 per cent. They've seen me at my most vulnerable and I trusted them completely with my well-being.

Academic study

Over and above the questions and discussion provided, I don't think I've got too much else to add to this topic, other than to say that if you're committed to your programme of study but feel it's becoming a source of stress/energy drain for you, perhaps try shifting your focus to another area such as where, how and when you study or the support or time out you need. Or find out if you're able to take a term off while you sort out some other areas of your life that are impacting on your ability to study at this time.

Aesthetics and living environment

Use the questions provided to guide your actions and stay focused on what you can control or change, and shift your focus away from what you're unable to influence.

Financial matters

Another short one. If you need professional advice to help you to sort out your finances, then seek it out and get some help.

Relationships

Everyone will have different challenges to face if their relationship (or singledom) is a source of stress. The questions provided have been designed to assist you in identifying what you may be feeling at this time, and why, when it comes to your relationship (or lack of one).

If you feel that you may be creating some of the stress you're experiencing in your relationship, hopefully some of the ideas we've covered already around behavioural fine-tuning will help you.

It's important too when we look at our relationships that we explore them carefully from two perspectives: ours and theirs. Sometimes we can become narrow in our vision and only see our own issues. We seek to assign blame and the rest is history as they say.

There are many great resources and experts out there that specialize in this topic, so seek them out and use them. Then you'll know that any decision you make is an informed one, rather than an emotional or reactive one.

Social conforms

Use the questions provided to guide your thoughts on this topic and then use previous sections around your own and other people's behaviours, rewriting internal programming, etc. to decide on what action to take.

Family

Another one that fits in the section on your own and other people's behaviour. Review your responses to the questions for this area and focus your energy on what you can control or influence in this situation. And seek out professional guidance as required.

Community

Do use your answers to the questions as your guide to action. Your local library or Citizens' Advice Bureau will have information about what's going on in your local area when it comes to community work, and so will your friends and neighbours. Therefore if you want to get more involved, find out what's going on in your local area.

A final word

As you read this book, I have no way of knowing where you stand with regard to your levels of stress, energy depletion or burnout. But regardless of where you feel you're currently at, I would like to encourage you to view it as being nothing more than a squashed bug on the windscreen of your life. By all means take it seriously and give it the attention it deserves, but like all squashed bugs, view it as being transitory, not set in stone.

If you complete the exercises in this book and develop and follow through with your Action Plan, you will start to notice a difference in terms of how you're feeling about yourself and your life. Nothing is a fixed state unless we choose it to be. Everything moves, shifts and evolves, and so do we.

I mention this because this mindset is an important one to adopt from the beginning. You have to be willing to take action and to believe that you can make the changes you want to make. It also helps to view what you're experiencing as an opportunity to learn and grow, not the end of life as you know it. There is a light at the end of the tunnel, and I'm shining it right at you.

And if for some reason you fall off along the way, don't worry. Learn from it, get back on the horse again, and keep moving forward. Don't beat yourself up about it. It's a waste of energy, which defeats the object of what you're trying to achieve here. You're human and these things happen, so let it go.

Don't worry about what other people may say or think either, or continually relive 'if only' and 'what if' scenarios in your mind. And let go of any anger, frustration or feelings of shame and embarrassment. All these things are a waste of energy. The past is the past. Learn from it and let it go. The rest of your life can start today if you choose it to.

I often say that I view my own experience of burnout as being one of the most enlightening experiences that I've ever had. It taught me a lot about myself and what's really important to me. It focused my work and my mind, and led me to a place where I am now able to help others. It was a gift – a necessary squashed bug if you like – that I had to experience and move beyond in order to have the life, and the wonderful opportunities, that I now have.

My wish for you as I close is that you find the tools and ideas contained within this book of use to you, as you set out on your own journey of discovery. You are in transition to a new place in your life. A happier and more content place, with a greater sense of who you are, what you want and why. You will grow at every level and transform yourself into something quite beautiful as you reach the other side; of that I'm sure. My heartfelt best wishes and words of encouragement go with you on your journey.

Further reading

Byrne, Rhonda, *The Secret*. Hillsboro, Oregon, USA, Beyond Words Publishing, 2006.

Carlson, Neil, *et al.*, *Psychology: The Science of Behaviour*. UK, Pearson Education Limited, 2000.

Carter, R., *Mapping the Mind*. London, Orion Publishing Group, 1999.

Church, Matt, *High Life 24/7*. Sydney, Australia, ABC Books, 2004.

Ford, Debbie, *The Dark Side of the Light Chasers*. New York, Riverhead Books, 1998.

Froggatt, Wayne, *Managing Stress in the Workplace with Rational Effectiveness Training*. New Zealand, 2004. http://www.rational.org.nz/orgs/workstress.htm

Girdano, Daniel, *et al.*, *Controlling Stress and Tension*. Massachusetts, USA, Pearson Education Company, 6th edn, 2001.

Goleman, Daniel, *Working With Emotional Intelligence*. London, Bloomsbury, 1998.

Gorkin, Mark, *The Four Stages of Burnout*. n.p., n.d. http://www.stressdoc.com

Hansen, Dr Sven, *Mastering Stress*. New Zealand, David Bateman Ltd, 2006.

Hartley, Anne, *Love the Life You Live*. NSW, Australia, Hart Publishing Pty Ltd, 2000.

Helpguide, *Burnout: Signs, Symptoms and Prevention*. USA, n.d. http://www.helpguide.org/mental/burnout_signs_symptoms.htm

Huther, Gerald, *The Compassionate Brain*. Massachusetts, USA, Shambhala Publications Inc., 2004.

Igodan, Chris O., and Newcomb, L. H., 'Are You Experiencing Burnout?', *US Journal of Extension*, vol. 24, no. 1, 1986. http://www.joe.org

Mayo Clinic, *Stress: Unhealthy Response to the Pressures of Life*. USA, n.d. http://www.mayoclinic.com/health/stress/SR00001

Morris, Charles G., and Maisto, Albert A., *Psychology: An Introduction*. New Jersey, USA, Prentice-Hall, 10th edn, 1999.

Overton, A., *Stress Less*. New Zealand, Random House, 2005.

Selby, Anna, *The Ancient and Healing Art of Chinese Herbalism*. London, Hamlyn, 1998.

Spradlin, Scott, *Don't Let Your Emotions Run Your Life*. Oakland, CA, USA, New Harbinger Publications Inc., 2003.

University of Passau, *Burnout*. Passau, Germany, n.d. http://www.fmi.uni-passau.de/worterklaerungen/burnout.html

Warren, Eve, and Toll, Caroline, *The Stress Workbook*. London, Nicholas Brealey Publishing Ltd, 1993.

Website

Conflict Resolution Network
http://www.crnhq.org/index.html

Index